Sustaining Leadership

Finding Your Path Through Self-Care

Gage E. Paine, Ph.D.

ISBN: 9798704332381
Front Cover Images: 123rf.com/MariaTkach
Additional Images: 123rf.com/YuttanaJaowattana, SamWordley,
Fizkes, Milkos, DmitryRukhlenko, SergiiSverdielov

EMERGING
INK SOLUTIONS
Kara Scrivener, Editor
www.emergingink.com

Notice: The information in this book is true and complete to the best of our knowledge. It is offered without guarantee on the part of the author, the editor/formatter, or the book's press. The author disclaims all liability in connection with the use of this book.

To the countless people who taught me leadership and yoga and who
inspired me to combine the two.

Table of Contents

Leadership and Yoga?

Introduction

The question comes in different forms. Sometimes it's asked by people who want to achieve something called "work-life balance." Other times, it's buried in a hopeful question about work load or about having a family; or maybe it comes disguised as a comment about stress. Whatever the details of the inquiry however, the underlying question is actually this – what does it take to sustain the challenging work of leadership?

Oh sure, educational credentials, experience, applicable skills, and prospective career paths are part of the conversation, but the most common kind of inquiry by far isn't about any of those things. No matter how the question is posed, at its core, the questioner wants to know:

- How do I maintain energy to be a leader over the long-term?

- How do I pursue challenging goals?

- Do I have the mental fortitude to be a living, breathing human while leading a complex organization or community?

What does it take to practice a kind of sustainable leadership that can serve people? This book is my answer to that question.

In my experience, it isn't about time management skills or finding the perfect system for organizing your workflow, though both are important. It's not a one-size-fits-all method or a great app. No, I've come to believe it's something simpler and more profound than all the latest techniques and methods.

The way to sustain your leadership over a career is to understand and practice self-care *as* a leadership skill.

Self-care is a popular topic these days. Unfortunately, the way it is often presented can make one feel as if it is yet another area of our lives in which we have failed if we are feeling tired and burned out. The images of women (usually) sitting in beautiful spaces with a soothing drink, looking out a window at a vista or something in soft focus, create an ideal that few of us can achieve.

Self-care as a leadership skill is not about finding time in an already busy schedule for a spa day or learning how to cook healthy meals on a regular basis, though, again, those certainly don't hurt. Understanding self-care as a leadership skill is a completely different way of thinking about the concept.

Conceptualizing self-care as an integral skill is a way of ritualizing it so that you learn to move through your day without feeling it is a burden you have to accomplish. For leaders, self-care is not a break from your leadership work. It is a way of leading and being a leader.

This book is based upon my experiences practicing, studying, and teaching both leadership and yoga. In it, I explore practices from yoga that have made it possible for me to sustain my leadership roles in a healthy way over a long career. These practices allow me to be deeply invested in the results of the work we were doing while letting go of outcomes that were not within my realm of control.

Yoga practices allow me to grieve deeply with students and staff and still tend to all that came at me in my leadership roles, including serving as vice president in one of the largest universities in the country. These practices have taught me that it is possible to be a strong leader who is not a bully, a flexible supervisor who also stands firm on core values, and a high-energy pacesetter who works long hours when necessary, but who also knows how to enjoy other aspects of life.

The goal here is to understand self-care as a practice that leads to a type of leadership that is regenerative rather than harmful. It is understanding the truth behind the cliché, "Put on your own oxygen mask first." Leaders who cannot take care of themselves cannot effectively care for others. In other words, these self-care practices allow us to create sustainable leadership.

What Is Leadership?

Let's begin with some thoughts about leadership. There are many answers to the question 'what is leadership?' but for the purposes of this book, we'll base our discussion on five fundamental principles.

1. **We all have the potential to be leaders.** Some of us strive for leadership positions, some of us are appointed, and others have to be convinced to take on a formal role. Each of us has varying levels of expertise, but all leaders have areas that require improvement and growth. Some of us prefer to lead from behind the scenes rather than stand at a lectern, while others prefer to lead from the middle or without a title. All of us have the ability to make a difference in our communities and organizations, which may be the clearest definition of leadership there is. Once we decide we want to make a difference, we start to act in ways that become leadership.

2. **Caring about something beyond ourselves is what spurs us to leadership.** What do you care about? This idea of wanting to make a difference brings us to an important point from Larraine Matusak's *Finding Your Voice: Learning to Lead Anywhere You Want to Make a Difference*. Matusak teaches that true leadership is based in what we care about. When we find something important to us and we begin to act on that feeling, we start our leadership journey.

Caring about something other than ourselves enables us to see what needs doing and prompts us to step forward to do that thing. Caring about something is what enables us to take actions that make the world a better place. It drives us to take responsibility beyond the boundaries set by our position or job description to make sure our organizations and communities work and thrive. Sooner or later, others notice what you are doing and begin to follow your lead – in other words, they see you as a leader no matter your title.

3. **Effective leadership matters.** Organizations with poor leaders generally don't function as well as those with engaged and effective ones. Our organizations and communities need leaders who are willing to do the hard work of leadership. And that work is more than organizational and interpersonal in nature. It is intra-personal work. We need leaders who are self-aware and work to be healthy, whole-hearted people of integrity. Only then will their leadership be positive for their organizations or communities and for the people who are part of or connected to that organization/community. Parker Palmer puts it this way, "A leader shapes the ethos in which others must live, an ethos as light-filled as heaven or as shadowy as hell. A good leader is intensely aware of the interplay of inner shadow and light, lest the act of leadership do more harm than good" (p. 78).

4. **Leadership doesn't depend on title.** Healthy organizations have leaders throughout the organization. Great organizations work to develop leaders no matter their titles or job duties. It's the ability to see what needs improving combined with the willingness to commit to work that defines a leader. Organizations that reward rather than ignore or punish initiative, creativity, and responsibility for self and others are organizations that truly believe in leadership.

5. **Leadership is a partnership.** On a practical level, leaders have to work with others for there to be any meaningful leadership. The most effective leaders are the people who understand this reality and make an effort to support the people with whom they are working. Whether it's formal leadership where a supervisory relationship is at play or informal leadership with people engaging by choice, leaders who work to understand that each person brings skills and talents into the mix achieve the best results. People who are able to grasp the concept of leadership as a partnership can truly make a difference because they harness the motivation and capabilities of people.

The Leadership Yoga Workshop

In 1995, I began seeing a rheumatologist who diagnosed me with an auto-immune disorder. My symptoms and test results were so vague that my diagnosis had a non-name, Undifferentiated Connective Tissue Disease. None of my symptoms of joint pain and fatigue were enough to stop me from doing what I wanted to do, but there were times they hindered me from *wanting* to do things. While waiting to see if this amorphous disease became something more severe, my doctor told me that the most important steps I could take were to manage my stress and keep moving. He suggested yoga as a way to accomplish both tasks.

Knowing nothing about yoga, I did what I usually do when I want to learn about something: I read a book. In spite of its name, *The Idiot's Complete Guide to Yoga* turned out to be a great introduction. Eventually, I graduated to video tapes and CDs – yes, this was a while ago. At least now there is a wealth of online resources available for interested practitioners. Ultimately, I was brave enough to go to a class.

It was in a class designed specifically for beginners that I began to truly understand the benefits of yoga. It helped me manage the stiffness and pain in my body, but I learned more from yoga than simply how to move into the different postures. I didn't understand it at the time, but I was learning practices that would change the way I lead.

The joint pain and fatigue dissipated as mysteriously as they had first appeared. Doctors had no explanation for either onset or remission beyond, "Sometimes it happens that way." Luckily for me, my disease symptoms never came back. However, the lessons of yoga stayed with me. I have no doubt my yoga practice has helped me manage stress and taught me skills that have been useful in my daily life and work.

I began teaching undergraduate courses in leadership a few years after I began yoga. In 2002, I enrolled in a yoga teacher training program. I wasn't sure if I would ever teach yoga, but I wanted to deepen my practice. Subsequently, I completed a 200-hour teacher training course. At the time, I was working at Trinity University and used the chance to ask several campus colleagues who were already taking yoga if they would be interested in free yoga classes while I practiced what I had learned in my course. Unsurprisingly, they agreed and I began instructing.

As I proceeded to teach both my yoga and leadership classes, I realized that I was using some of the same words in each of them: strength, balance, flexibility, self-awareness, and continuous practice. And from that realization, the idea for the Leadership Yoga Workshop was born.

One of the founding principles of the course came from Matusak's book. The former university president and leadership scholar writes about an important leadership skill: risk-taking, explaining that "[r]isk-taking is definitely something that can be learned… In fact, the process is quite simple. Try new things. Be creative. Put yourself in positions that are slightly uncomfortable – stretch." In the Leadership Yoga Workshop, we take her literally. The workshop invites people to try positions that are often new, awkward, or even difficult and uncomfortable. And of course, we stretch ourselves.

Bringing the two practices together creates an interesting juxtaposition and generates reflection on both self-care and leadership practices.

What Is Yoga? And What Does It Have to Do with Leadership?

As we set the stage with leadership, it's also important to consider the practice of yoga. Let's begin with the word yoga and a bit of history about its practice. "The word Yoga is derived from the Sanskrit root *yuj* meaning to bind, join, attach and yoke, to direct and concentrate one's attention on, to use and apply. It also means union and communion" (Iyengar, p. 19). Yoga began in India with an oral tradition that is thought to be about 5,000 years old.

Approximately 2,000 years ago, the Indian sage Patanjali gathered the lessons of this oral tradition and wrote *The Yoga Sutras of Patanjali*, which constitutes a sort of philosophical guide for coping with the challenges of being human. While the practice of yoga focuses first, and for many people, only on the postures called *asanas* in the United States, there is more to yoga than learning to twist oneself into knots. It has been my experience that even if most people don't explore the full range of yoga experiences, those who practice yoga for any length of time gain benefits beyond the physical practice.

Yoga is not a religion in and of itself, though many people use its lessons and practices as a part of their own spiritual and religious customs. It's more accurate to describe it as a practice for understanding the ways in which the body, mind, and spirit are intertwined.

The physical practice of yoga, known as Hatha yoga, "was developed as a vehicle for meditation. The repertoire of Hatha yoga prepared the body, particularly the nervous system, of the ancient yogis for stillness, creating the necessary physical strength and stamina that allowed the mind to remain calm" (Carrico, p. 4). In my own experience, finding ways to keep my body, mind, and spirit healthy and in alignment have played an important role not only in my health, but in my leadership and in the longevity of my career.

The lessons I've learned from practicing, studying, and teaching yoga have been important to me in my practicing, studying, and teaching of leadership.

What Do Leadership and Yoga Have in Common?

Over time, leadership and yoga bring us face-to-face with who we are, warts and all. We learn what is easy for us to do and what is difficult. In different ways, each practice challenges us to be strong and flexible. But leadership and yoga are practices that require continuous work to improve and master. Both illustrate the adage, "The more you know, the more there is to learn." The two practices bring us new challenges and push us to do the work of learning from our experiences. Lastly, yoga and leadership remind us that the only way to learn something is to get up and practice. Neither leadership nor yoga are spectator sports. You have to learn by doing.

Leadership and yoga require us to be strong while learning to be strong. They help us learn balance and flexibility while pushing us off balance and showing us the ways in which we are tight or rigid. They require discipline and self-awareness to make any difference in ourselves and for people around us. Leadership and yoga push us to try something new, to put ourselves into uncomfortable positions, and to learn from the experience. In other words, to stretch ourselves.

When we first start yoga, many of us experience discomfort, even anxiety. Our mind tells us we can't do this. We feel uncoordinated or as if we are not flexible enough. Our body may chide us for having not been more active. We're forced to confront our fears of looking foolish, feeling awkward, or of not doing it correctly. And any one of those feelings and fears can show up just as easily when we start a new job, take on unfamiliar tasks, or accept a leadership role.

In both practices, there comes a point at the end of a session where it's necessary to stop and rest. In yoga, the final pose is designed to let the physical work you have done be absorbed into your body. It may be the single most important yoga pose in any practice.

In leadership, it is equally important to find times to stop and reflect so that the lessons you are learning are absorbed into your experience. That final pose, those moments of reflection, are places where change begins and growth occurs.

The Differences Between Leadership and Yoga

Of course, leadership and yoga are also different practices, so naturally, we spend time in the Leadership Yoga Workshop exploring ways the practices differ. For example, leadership is a relationship with others, a partnership with the rest of your team, one in which you are asked to be aware of the world around you, the people, the circumstances, and how effectively you are engaging with them. The measure of your success is the effectiveness with which you help a group achieve its goals and your ability to make that difference in the world around you.

Conversely, yoga is a practice for developing a relationship with yourself. In yoga class, the only person you pay attention to is yourself and your own experience. You do what you can, stop when you need to, and extend yourself when it is safe and healthy to do so. You learn to stretch and grow by paying attention to yourself, not by paying attention to or comparing yourself to others. Yes, you listen to the instructor if you are in a class. But you don't watch the other students to see what they are doing. You don't compare yourself to others or rank yourself along some continuum of good to bad or smooth to awkward.

In yoga class, we learn by paying attention to not only our physical experiences, but to our emotional and mental realities. Your practice is for you and you alone, and your measure of success is how you feel at the end of class rather than how you perform each pose or activity along the way.

The Purpose and Design of This Book

Yoga and leadership have much to teach us about ourselves on many levels. The lessons yoga has for us about self-awareness and its benefits as a practice of self-care are the concepts we hear about the most. On that level, yoga benefits us as people and as leaders. But yoga has lessons to teach leaders beyond self-care. It can support your aspiration to be an ethical leader who is able to act in accord with the highest of ideals. It provides leaders with tools to manage stress, listen more effectively, and move beyond the idea of "work-life balance" to the concept of an "integrated life."

Yoga works well as an extended metaphor for understanding what you (the leader) and your colleagues and partners experience as you strive to make a difference in your organizations and communities.

It's important to understand that this book is not going to teach you yoga. It is not a detailed study of the eightfold path of yoga, yoga postures, or yoga philosophy. We will cover a few poses in a very limited way to give you an idea of the work we do in the Leadership Workshop.

The focus, the *real* purpose of the book, is to distill from the workshop a series of practices and behaviors that will support your goal of developing a sustainable practice of leadership. Often, the workshop is a first introduction to yoga which leads students to try yoga classes and develop a yoga practice. For students who have taken yoga before, it adds a new dimension to their practice. But neither the workshop nor this book will prepare you to start your own yoga practice.

What this book is designed to do is to practice one of the most important lessons of yoga: taking our experiences in class ("on the mat") out into the world ("off the mat"). Lessons and practices I have developed that come from my years of yoga experiences have deepened my leadership practice. I hope they will support your appetite to make a difference in the world around you – whether you have a title or not.

The chapters loosely follow the general order of a yoga class with each chapter focusing on an aspect of practice. The first three chapters describe components of the first few minutes of a class – they are preparation for the work of the class.

The subsequent five chapters cover the various aspects most often illuminated in traditional Hatha Yoga classes. The last practice is based on the final posture in most yoga classes and brings the practice to a close. At the end of each chapter, I ask you to pause and reflect on your learning to better allow the lessons to be absorbed.

As you read through the following chapters, I encourage you to try the different exercises and think about ways to implement them throughout your day. Not all of the practices will suit everyone, but remember, these ideas are designed to *stretch* you. A willingness to try new ideas rather than assuming they won't work for you is an important exercise for your leadership skills and for life.

That being said, if you try something for a bit and find that it doesn't work, put it aside with no guilt. In class, we modify poses to adapt to differing levels of ability and experience. In the same way, feel free to modify any of the suggested practices. For example, if a pose calls for standing and that doesn't work for you, try it sitting down. No matter your ability, I encourage you to find a way to try something that pushes you a bit. Self-care as a leadership skill is all about individuality.

Our world needs people who are willing and able to make a difference. My hope is that this book will help you develop a leadership practice that is healthy, grounded, and sustainable so you can make a positive difference in the world far into the future.

Welcome to Leadership Yoga – practices for learning self-care as a leadership skill.

Preparation

The first few minutes of a yoga class are vital. They teach the necessity of preparation; that is, the time at the beginning dedicated for students to set aside everything they were doing before class and begin moving to a state of inner calm. Creating a simple way to leave distractions behind and shift mentally to yoga as class begins changes the way we participate. And this is equally true for an academic class or professional development workshop.

James Lang, a contributing writer for *The Chronicle of Higher Education,* states, "The opening five minutes offer us a rich opportunity to capture the attention of students and prepare them for learning. They walk into classes trailing all the distractions of their complex lives — the many wonders of their smartphones, the distractions of their complex lives, the question of what to have for lunch. Their bodies may be stuck in a room with us for the required time period, but their minds may be somewhere else entirely."

The way instructors or facilitators introduce a subject can either engage students and participants or convince them that the topic will be uninteresting and unworthy of their attention. It's why authors stress over the opening lines and paragraphs of their books. This idea of a space at the beginning of a gathering, however, runs counter to the culture of most organizations and communities.

Often, when it's time for the meeting to start, we simply begin. At best, we do a quick check-in to see how people are doing, but then we dive right into the agenda. The exception to this norm is faith-based organizations, which often start with some sort of prayer or meditation. While those practices have a different primary purpose, they also have the benefit of refocusing participants' attention as well as quieting the room.

Some instructors practice what is known as *contemplative pedagogy*, which is defined by the Columbia University Center for Teaching and Learning as "an approach to teaching and learning with the goal of encouraging deep learning through focused attention, reflection, and heightened awareness." Their website addresses the benefits of implementing contemplative practices in traditional teaching methods, suggesting, "The integration of contemplative practices encourages instructors and learners to focus on the present moment, to fully engage in teaching and learning, and to achieve focus and attention in the classroom."

The same benefits apply to our study and practice of leadership. Focusing our attention on the task at hand, fully engaging with the people with whom we are working, and listening deeply to what others are saying and to what we are feeling and thinking are contemplative practices that can increase our effectiveness as leaders. Additionally, these practices and others require us to slow down and attend to what is happening around us and within ourselves. This is a self-care practice for leaders.

Preparation focuses on three practices that are common to many yoga classes, including those I teach. In a usual hour or hour and a half-long yoga class, it is customary for these first three practices to be intertwined and to take no more than five or ten minutes. And yet, I will spend a full chapter on each one because those first few minutes set the tone for everything that follows. Those initial moments provide participants the opportunity to make the mental shift from the everyday world to the present moment. Well-thought-out beginnings set the stage for what happens next.

The same principle applies to the work of leaders. Whether you are leading a meeting or making a presentation or set of remarks before your colleagues, how you begin sets the tone for what happens next. This is more than setting an agenda or plan for the session. It is a thoughtful invitation into the work and purpose of the meeting. Taking time at the beginning to help participants understand what is expected of them supports their engagement in the work to be done. Acknowledging the expertise in the room creates an expectation that everyone needs to bring their attention and talent to the task at hand. Making it possible for others to make a shift from the busyness of a day to collaborative time is part of leadership work, work that is often omitted in the rush of the day to day.

The principle of paying attention to beginnings also applies to the start of a new job, the development of a new program, or an individual meeting with a colleague. Taking even a few minutes to prepare yourself, to engage in these first three practices at the start of these types of experiences will make a difference in the way you feel as you proceed in your work and relationships. It will support your leadership. It will help you stay connected to what is important and provide focus to the work you are doing.

The following three chapters focus on three practices and describe the preparations one should take when it comes to classes and meetings. Each of them is a self-care practice by itself. Finding ways to exercise the first three practices on a regular basis will change the way you feel physically, mentally, and emotionally. They won't make a difficult day easier, but based on my experience, they *will* help you manage the difficult day more effectively so you feel better when the day is over.

Beginnings set the stage for the future. It is worth taking time to start well.

Practice 1

Breathing Well

At my very first yoga class, I found myself lying on the floor of a room in the Texas Union on the campus of The University of Texas at Austin. I was breathing. That was it. Just breathing. Not what I thought I would be doing in a yoga class, though if I had stopped and thought about it, I actually had no idea what a yoga class was comprised of. The Union offered a six-week program as part of their informal classes, and a friend and I decided to give it a try. I don't think we ever went back. Despite our limited experience, I do remember something the instructor told us: most people have forgotten how to breathe correctly.

This was certainly a surprising notion. It had never occurred to me that there are correct and incorrect ways to breathe. The teacher explained that in the United States, most people breathe shallowly, breathing only into their chests and using just the upper parts of their lungs. I remember her saying, "Next time you are seated in a theater or lecture hall, look down the row and you can see it. Chests rising and falling, no one is breathing deeply." Something about that image caught my attention. I don't examine people's breathing regularly, though I have tried the look-down-the-row idea; she was right. Most people do breathe shallowly. From that point forward, I found myself on occasion paying attention to my breath even though it was probably ten years before I took another class and began to understand more deeply what she was trying to teach us.

One of the important ways yoga is different from other forms of exercise is its emphasis on the breath. In the practice of yoga, we work to understand, pay attention to, and use our breath to support our movements. For practitioners who delve deep into yoga, there's even a specific component called *pranayama*, which focuses entirely on the breath. Like many instructors, when I teach a yoga class, we begin by spending the first few moments focusing on our breathing. Yoga has taught me exactly what James Lang, referenced earlier, writes about.

Taking the time to focus participants on their breath at the start of a class gives people a chance to leave the outside world outside. It gives them the opportunity to come to class mentally and emotionally in the same way they came to class physically.

Like the changing of clothes or the unrolling of a yoga mat, observing our breath is a signal to ourselves to change our focus, to begin the process of attending to what is happening within the room and within ourselves.

Understanding the importance of and developing the habit of being aware of our breathing is the start of a true yoga practice. And in my experience, it is also the start of coming to a deeper understanding of ourselves and, consequently, our leadership style, skills, and purpose. This is why our first practice is a focus on the breath.

The Calming and Energizing Effects of Breath

Whether we actively pay attention to the correlation between our breathing and the way we feel, we instinctively understand the connection. After all, when someone is upset or excited, we exhort them to take a deep breath. In a group that's struggling with a task or embroiled in a difficult conversation, we might say, "Let's all take a breather and come back to this topic in a moment." When we are ready to try something unknown or a bit difficult, we draw a deep breath to fortify ourselves before we start. What is a sigh but a deep exhalation? "Whew!" is as much an expression of relief as it is an exhalation. When we fall exhausted into a chair, we exhale. But until I started practicing and studying yoga, I didn't understand there was a scientific reason for our innate reactions.

Try this for a moment. Take a deep breath and hold it for as long as you reasonably can. Now, let it go and allow your breathing to return to normal. Think for a moment about the way you felt. It wasn't relaxing to keep holding your breath, was it? In fact, if you hold your breath too long, it can cause anxiety. After all, we need to keep breathing. When your breathing has returned to normal, try it a different way. Take a deep, deep breath, imagining air filling your lungs completely and then let your breath out completely in whatever way feels good to you. Notice how you feel compared to when you hold your breath. An exhalation is calming, not anxiety-inducing.

More is happening here than the need for air. Our nervous system, which is connected to our brain and therefore to our emotions, influences our physical being. According to an article in *Scientific American*, "[W]hen you are feeling frightened, in pain, or tense and uncomfortable, your breathing speeds up and becomes shallower. The sympathetic nervous system, which is responsible for the body's various reactions to stress, is now activated." Your breathing speeds up in response to outside stimuli to prepare your body for action. In the same way, when your breathing is shallow and tense, your body is ready for action even if there is no threat or danger. It's tiring living on the precipice of constant awareness and action.

Conversely, "When you are feeling calm and safe, at rest or engaged in a pleasant social exchange, your breathing slows and deepens. You are under the influence of the parasympathetic nervous system which produces a relaxing effect" (André, "Proper Breathing Brings Better Health"). And you can trigger that calming effect by changing how you breathe.

Several years ago, I was sitting in my car waiting for my husband to come out of an auto shop. As is often the case with car repairs, this was an unexpected trip inserted into an already busy day. I remember that the longer he stood in line inside, the more anxious I grew. I had things to do. Important things, I'm sure. Suddenly, I tuned to my breath. It was tight, shallow, and much too rapid for someone simply sitting in a stationary vehicle. I changed my breathing, deliberating taking longer, slower, deeper breaths. And soon, I was no longer feeling anxious. It didn't make the line go any faster. It didn't make my to-do list shorter or less important. Changing my breathing simply made me feel better. And it kept me from passing on my anxiety to my husband by complaining about something neither of us had any control over. I used my breathing to help me manage my response to the situation.

This is why telling someone who is stressed to take a breath is only half of the equation. It is the exhalation that is actually calming. Yes, we need to take a deep breath, but we also need to let it out slowly and completely. Then, do it all over again. Deep, slow breathing is one of the best methods to manage stress and anxiety in the moment. As yoga teacher and author Donna Farhi writes in *The Breathing Book: Good Health and Vitality Through Essential Breath Work*, modern science is proving what ancient health traditions have taught for centuries: "when we breathe well, we create the optimum conditions for health and well-being. And when we don't, we lay the foundation for illnesses such as heart disease and high blood pressure" (p. 87).

Research studies have taught us that paying attention to our breathing causes most people to slow it down and deepen it, which triggers the parasympathetic nervous system; thus, it becomes soothing. Breathing exercises can help with insomnia and in-the-moment stressors, such as public speaking, chronic anxiety, and the minor physical tension that comes from stress (André, "Proper Breathing Brings Better Health").

But relieving stress doesn't always mean relaxation. There are yoga breathing practices that can help us increase our energy, raise our heart rate, and leave us feeling energized. Practiced knowledgeably, they don't lead to anxiety as rapid breathing or hyperventilating can. By bringing oxygen into the body in a way that triggers the sympathetic nervous system, breathing practices such as Breath of Fire and Lion's Breath bring energy to our bodies and relieves stress simultaneously.

Breathing in Yoga

In a yoga class, we don't simply move from one *asana* (posture) to another. Instead, as we change positions, we match our breathing to the movements. We inhale deeply as we open our chests through backbends. These are energizing moves. We exhale fully as we bend forward into a deeply relaxing posture. When a pose is challenging, shifting our attention to our breath can help us find a way to relax into it. By noticing when our breathing is tight, we can learn when we are trying to force something to happen. Subsequently, we discover our limits.

Becoming aware of our breathing can teach us the difference between a healthy effort and a harmful strain. Holding a difficult pose while breathing smoothly, deeply, and calmly helps us become physically and psychologically stronger while teaching us the difference between striving and learning. When the lessons we learn in yoga class begin to influence our behavior outside of class, we are able to experience the true depth and power of yoga.

Yoga teaches us more than the ability to move our bodies in new and challenging ways. It helps us discover ways to handle difficult situations and overwhelming emotions. Pausing to pay attention to our breathing allows us to be present and to choose how we react. When we concentrate on each aspect of the breathing process, we can let go of the past and the future and be focused on the moment.

Being able to stay calm is, in and of itself, a useful skill. When you are stressed, tired, or concerned, deep breathing is both energizing and calming. In the middle of a long day, standing up, stretching slightly, and taking a deep breath is refreshing. Yoga's focus on breathing can help us increase our ability to focus on our work, be present for the people and tasks around us, and manage the energy needed to get through a challenging day. This is self-care.

Leadership and Breathing

A friend, mentor, and former supervisor once shared with me an essential lesson she learned while serving as Dean of Students at a large complex university. During a conversation with the university president, she was instructed clearly and concisely to "count to ten before you arrest a student."

Arresting a student is an extreme, but certainly not unheard-of example of the difficult and urgent decisions leaders make, often on a daily basis. One of the realities of having a formal leadership position is that people look to you in times of crisis and want answers immediately. After all, leaders are supposed to be decisive, aren't they? They are expected to have the ability to find the right answers to complex and urgent problems. These expectations can make it easy to jump into making quick decisions.

Making a decision, *any* decision, takes away the immediate pressure on a leader and often the responsibility from other people in the organization. And yet, it is rare that we face a decision that truly needs an instant answer. In my experience, the university president was right. Our decisions often benefit from counting to ten. Or in other words, taking a breath.

Breathing as part of our leadership practice has many facets. Counting to ten before you react to the emotion – yours or others' – in a situation is one example. I also recommend that as you count to ten, you actually stop for a moment and focus on your breathing. Counting to ten while gritting your teeth isn't what is needed here. Counting to ten and allowing for one full inhalation and one full exhalation will help you be calmer and more clear-headed. You'll be more receptive to ideas and have a steadier resolve.

Allowing yourself to take a deep breath, or better yet, two or three, when everyone and everything is pressuring you to act now is an important leadership skill. That pause helps leaders make better choices in tough circumstances and to feel more confident in their decisions. It may help you decide whether or not an immediate pronouncement is called for. After all, some decisions are better when there has been some time for reflection. But even in an emergency, a few seconds to take a deep breath helps us react with clearer hearts and minds.

Taking time to focus on the breath throughout a normally busy day is important as well and is yet another example of self-care. If more of us took the time to pause momentarily during the day to give ourselves time to focus on our breath, we would not only immediately feel better, but we are more likely to feel better at the end of the day. Take a *breather* and walk outside for five minutes between meetings; stand up from your computer, open a window, and focus on your breathing; after throwing groceries into the trunk, sit in your car quietly and observe your breathing.

Developing simple ways to remind ourselves to breathe deeply throughout the day can help us be healthy and strong physically, mentally, and emotionally. Understanding the way we breathe and using breathing practices to support ourselves and our leadership is our first self-care practice because it is the foundation of everything we do.

Just a few seconds of focused deep breathing can support your leadership practice all day, every day.

Questions for Reflection and Learning

✸ What do you already know about your breathing?

Take some time to reflect on what you know about your breathing. Someone who has asthma might have a great deal of knowledge about their breathing while another with acute allergies might only become aware of their breathing during certain times of the year. Some of us may notice our breathing only upon exertion. Athletes of all levels pay attention to their breath as a way of understanding their effort or as a way of enabling them to do strenuous activities with less risk. If you've never had to pay attention to your breath before, note that.

✸ As a leader, have you ever noticed your breathing during stressful situations? If so, how, if at all, did your breathing inform your action as a leader?

✸ How Do You Breathe?

Spend some time over the next few days learning about your breath. Set a timer for 30 minutes from now and work to forget it. When it signals you, stop and notice your breath at that moment. Was it slow and deep or tense and shallow? Don't judge yourself for your answer; this is a practice of noticing and learning. End the session with a long, slow, deep breath.

Now, set your timer for another interval, perhaps an hour from now or 90 minutes. It's your choice. When the timer signals, repeat the steps above.

At the end of the day, ask yourself what you learned from this inquiry. Repeat this practice each day for three or four days and keep a record of what you notice and learn.

Breathing Practices

Focus on the Breath

Now that you have spent some time learning about your breathing patterns, you can begin to use your breath to support your health and wellbeing throughout the day. You can also use your breath to support your leadership.

Create reminders for yourself to stop at various points in the day – perhaps using the same system as above. This time though, choose how you will breathe for the next moment. The simplest way is to slow down. Take one or two slow, deep breaths that fill your lungs completely and exhale just as fully.

Pay attention throughout the day. If you find yourself feeling tense, take a deep breath. You can do this in the middle of a meeting with no one the wiser. If you find yourself feeling sleepy, take a few deep breaths with a forward bend. While this won't work in the meeting, you can try it before entering the conference room. The addition of the forward bend adds some energy to the mix and we'll explore why in a later chapter.

Practice 2

Paying Attention

It was six or seven years into my career, that I first learned an important leadership lesson – self-awareness makes a difference. I supervised staff of varying levels, ranging from student Resident Assistants to staff members who were not only older than I was, but who had been in their jobs for a couple of decades, during that time. I learned something from each of them. But none of them taught me as critical a lesson as the person I hired at this point.

This colleague taught me that much of what I knew about working in a professional environment came, not from classes, books, or workshops, or even from supervisors or mentors, but from watching my parents do their jobs, both of whom had professional careers. I was completely unaware of the lessons I had learned growing up because they were just in the air around me, which meant this staff member, whose background was different from mine, was correct in their assertion that I hadn't been clear in my expectations. I thought I was expecting behaviors everyone knew. It had never occurred to me that I needed to explain some things. My lack of self-awareness about my own experiences caused problems for both of us.

At the start of a yoga class, as we begin to focus on our breathing, we also introduce the important yoga practice of paying attention, of being self-aware. We exercise self-awareness throughout a yoga class when we listen to what our bodies have to tell us as we move through different postures. For students who have been practicing for some time, the act of kicking off their shoes, coming into the studio, and rolling out the yoga mat begins the process of paying attention.

Whether we are standing or in a seated position, begin with our breath. And it is through our breath that we become self-aware in that moment and take the time to check in physically with our bodies. We notice aches, pains, points of tightness, as well as any ways that we are physically uncomfortable. Simultaneously, we note the ways that we feel good in our body.

Perhaps you discern that the headache which has plagued you all morning has receded. Or you realize that you are seated cross-legged on the floor and it's comfortable for the first time. It's a time to listen to what your body has to tell you about your sense of physical self. You can also check in with how you feel emotionally, to observe your mental state.

Are you relieved to have gotten to class or frustrated at the traffic that made it stressful to drive? Are you irritated about something that happened during the day? Maybe you are eager to get started. Whatever your experience is, taking this time at the beginning of class is part of the yoga practice, but it is also part of a larger practice in self-awareness.

What Is Self-awareness?

Merriam-Webster.com defines self-awareness rather simply as "an awareness of one's own personality or individuality." This is subsequently translated into a deeper knowledge of one's character, feelings, and motives. Psychologists Shelley Duval and Robert Wiklund are credited with developing the theory of self-awareness in 1972. According to their theory, focusing attention on ourselves allows us to evaluate and compare our current behavior to our internal standards and values. They understood self-awareness as a mechanism of self-control because the comparison of ourselves with these internal standards allows us to change our behaviors, evaluate whether we are making the right choices in pursuit of our goals, and make choices aligned with our values.

Self-awareness, one of four components of Emotional Intelligence, is defined in *Primal Leadership: Realizing the Power of Emotional Intelligence* as "[…] having a deep understanding of one's emotions, as well as one's strengths and limitations and one's values and motives. People with strong self-awareness are realistic […] and they are honest with themselves about themselves" (p. 40). In the book, the authors incorporate this concept of self-awareness into the realm of leadership, writing, "Self-aware leaders also understand their values, goals, and dreams. They know where they are headed and why. They're attuned to what 'feels right' to them." The authors go on to say, "[P]erhaps the most telling (though least visible) sign of self-awareness is a propensity for self-reflection and thoughtfulness. Self-aware people typically find time to reflect quietly, often off by themselves, which allows them to think things over rather than act impulsively" (p. 40).

Yoga gives us the opportunity to practice self-awareness at the physical level. Discipline in the art of yoga asks us to pay attention to our reactions as we move while challenging us to understand our physical reactions: this pose is really difficult; my body doesn't move this way; or I can do this. It also invites us to move beyond physical aspects to learn from our mental and emotional reactions to the practice: I don't like this pose; I feel awkward; this pose makes me uncomfortable; wow, this pose feels great.

Taking time in class to pay attention to both our physical and mental/emotional experiences and reactions to different postures improves our experience. Noticing our reactions to the movements and whether or not they change during class or throughout the week is a way to deepen our learning. Being willing and able to let ourselves experience the emotions that we feel during class also deepens our learning and is an introduction to the practice of reflection.

Paying attention to our experiences and our reactions to those experiences during class helps develop skills for paying attention outside of class. It increases our self-awareness and, therefore, our understanding of the ways we react to the twists and turns of life. The more self-aware we are, the more effective we are at deciding how to respond to our circumstances; we are subsequently more likely to be consistent at matching our actions to our values.

On the mat, there are always postures that are difficult. Sometimes, poses we feel we have mastered suddenly become challenging again for what seems like no reason at all. Introspection forces us to face those changes with equanimity. Paying attention out of class doesn't mean everything is easy, but it does help us learn and grow when things are difficult. In fact, self-awareness can make life more challenging because we aren't ignoring or minimizing what we are feeling. However, research shows that self-awareness is an overall benefit because it helps us exercise self-control which contributes to our ability to choose our actions rather than thoughtlessly react.

Acting Consciously

Even the person who says, "I don't like routine. I'm all about doing things differently" has something they don't want anyone to modify. Change can be threatening to many people and evoke strong feelings, including anger. Anger can actually be a grief response to the altering of our world and worldview. Change, even when welcomed, often means we have to give up something and that loss can result in grieving. Understanding the anger as an expression of grief gave me an opportunity to change the way I responded to colleagues who were angry about whatever we were facing at the time.

Most of us prefer to initiate change rather than have it imposed upon us. A practice of self-awareness can help each of us understand our emotional responses and the responses of others to change, stressful situations, and difficult decisions. When we are more accurate at identifying responses, ours and others', we are more likely to take care of ourselves and support others in the way they most need to be supported.

The art of yoga challenges us to concentrate on the feelings we bring into class and notice how they shift as we move through various postures. If we are able to acknowledge and understand the emotion we are truly feeling – grief expressed as anger, fear expressed as apathy, a need for calm rather than an unwillingness to try something new – we are more likely to choose effective ways to respond to situations. Understanding and fully experiencing our own emotions is one step toward understanding and responding with compassion to others. A learned self-awareness when coupled with breath techniques can make an individual more confident in the difficult decisions they make. In times of crisis, being heart-healthy and self-aware can help us manage our emotions while we support others as they experience their own reactions.

"Self-aware people tend to act consciously (rather than react passively) and tend to be in good psychological health and to have a positive outlook on life. They also have a great depth of experience and are likely to be more compassionate" (Zhu, "Why Self-awareness Matters and How to Be More Self-aware"). The more easily we can determine our responses to the situations around us, the more we can find ways to respond with compassion.

A practice of self-awareness, supported by deep breathing, can help us develop the resiliency necessary to meet the challenges of life and leadership. When we experience strong emotions, the skills learned on the mat can help us choose our response. By exercising self-awareness, we give ourselves the ability to select options that align with our values and ideals while effectively meeting the needs of the people around us.

Heart-Healthy

Yoga is designed to work all of your muscles rather than a particular group or type of muscle. So naturally, this includes your heart. Of course, any movement works your heart as it pumps blood through your circulatory system, but the benefits of yoga far surpass those of conventional exercise.

Yoga teachers often encourage students to move into postures from their heart center, where the Self is found. We bring our hands together in front of our chest to focus our attention on our hearts, to help us concentrate on the way different positions make us feel. It's not unusual for people to be surprised by an upwelling of emotion, even tears, during a yoga class. Because our focus is turned inward as we practice yoga, we have the ability to pay close attention to the movements of our body and how they change from day-to-day or throughout the class.

Self-awareness as a Leader

As I mentioned in the Introduction, one of the ways the practices of yoga and leadership differ is that leaders have to pay attention to the people and circumstances around them while simultaneously observing themselves and their own reactions. In the same way, self-awareness is a practice that prepares us to be more aware of the people around us.

In the Leadership Yoga Workshop, we often practice partner yoga, which is exactly what it sounds like. It's an opportunity to practice poses with a partner. Partner yoga is two people creating poses together as equal participants, even if their actual abilities vary.

In the workshop, we only do two or three postures, but even 15 minutes or so of practice reveals to participants the essential elements of working with a partner while illustrating an important leadership skill and the benefits of collaboration. Partner work gives each individual the opportunity to stretch a bit further, the counterbalance of weight offering each person the opportunity to relax into new poses. It teaches us that we can do more than we think and that having a supportive partner helps us achieve results we otherwise would be unable to accomplish.

It's possible to get hurt or to hurt someone in partner yoga if we don't pay attention to some simple but essential elements. The same is true of leadership.

As you move through the postures or lead in any context, it's important to pay attention to your own abilities and boundaries. In yoga classes, rather than push through pain, we stop and ask the teacher for assistance or a way to modify a pose. When working with a partner, the same ideas apply. Awareness of our experience level, our feelings, and our boundaries is an important skill in working with a partner in yoga and everywhere else. In partner yoga and in leadership, being honest with yourself and with your colleagues about your skills and your abilities, or your energy at any particular point in time, is a critical first step to being an effective leader. Pushing ourselves into areas where we lack skills has the potential to cause harm to ourselves and to others.

Another important element in both partner yoga and leadership, not surprisingly, is communication. For example, while working with a partner in alternating forward bends, each partner needs to clearly and immediately speak up when they have reached the furthest point of a comfortable stretch. The other partner needs to be ready to pause instantly. That's the simple part, because, of course, those places of comfort and discomfort change with each iteration of the stretch. Speaking about our own and listening to our partner's needs requires deep and trustworthy communication.

In leadership work, our ability to honestly communicate direction and boundaries and to listen to the needs and ideas of others, is one of the most crucial skills for effective leadership work.

This brings us to trust. There are many poses in partner yoga we can't do without the support of a companion. If partners don't hold each other with strength, gentleness, and the right amount of tension and support, they'll both topple over. If one person isn't able or willing to be vulnerable, to admit the need for support, the partnership fails. "If either or both of you are fighting to stay in control of your own independent balance, you will struggle. Someone always seems to be pulling a little too much or not enough, as if you war working against each other" (Carrol, C. & L. Kimata, p. 96). To develop organizational and community interdependence, members need to trust in others.

Lastly, partner yoga works best when there's bit of fun involved. A willingness to laugh when things don't go well. An ability to play with a new idea even if it's awkward and doesn't seem to quite work out as it should. Laughter is a necessary component of a partnership. Our self-awareness supports our self-confidence, even in a task that is new and awkward, and through both it creates the ability to laugh at ourselves and our own goofs.

The idea that it's self-awareness that makes true partnership possible is a wonderful paradox. Yoga teaches us ways to pay attention to our own experiences in great depth and on multiple levels. Understanding our own experiences and abilities is a skill that helps us honor the experience of others. And that is an essential part of being a leader.

Paying attention to what we value and believe and what we are thinking and feeling is the first step. The second step then is paying attention to what we are doing and whether or not these are in alignment. An active practice of paying attention, of being self-aware is part of the both self-care and leading with integrity.

Questions for Reflection

❁ How well do you know yourself?

This is a fundamentally difficult question, especially since self-awareness isn't a one-and-done practice. Over time, our skills and abilities grow as do our willingness and our ability to acknowledge our own strengths and weaknesses. One way to begin to answer this question is to take one or more of the different personality assessments or values clarification exercises that are available. Some are available online; others need to be administered by and discussed with a trained professional. Each of them has different purposes and adherents, but all help us understand our reactions to various situations and are helpful tools of learning.

If you have a trusted friend or know someone who has training in the assessment you took or exercise you completed, I challenge you to sit down, share your insights with them, and ask for feedback.

❁ What are your assumptions and unspoken expectations?

Take some time to think about or write out lessons you have learned over the past few years. What do those lessons teach you about some of the assumptions you carry with you, the values that underly your work, and the unspoken expectations you have for yourself or others?

Taking time to learn, understand, and articulate the ways these assumptions, values, and expectations connect to your actions will help you decide if you need to change behaviors. Perhaps you may not need to change what you do, but you will want to alter how you explain your decision-making to others. Understanding what makes you act and react the ways you do is an integral part of self-awareness and requires time and attention on a regular basis.

Self-awareness Exercises

Pay Attention

Pay attention to your physical, mental, and emotional state throughout the day. Notice what makes you happy and relaxed. Acknowledge when you become tense, upset, or tired. The act of paying attention teaches you about yourself. It helps you understand the causes of the different behaviors you exhibit throughout the day. It also allows you to step outside yourself for a moment to choose your actions and reactions to your experiences and your emotions. It helps you feel "attuned to what is right," as Goleman describes it.

Morning Pages

I'll say this right now: the concept of self-care as a leadership skill will *not* add to your to-do list, but this practice will. However, I challenge you to give it a try, because it is, by far, one of the most important practices I have adopted. The practice is Julia Cameron's Morning Pages, made famous in her book *The Artist's Way*. The practice itself is simple. Here's the description from her website:

"Morning Pages are three pages of longhand, stream of consciousness writing, done first thing in the morning. *There is no wrong way to do Morning Pages*– they are not high art. They are not even 'writing.' They are about anything and everything that crosses your mind – and they are for your eyes only. Morning Pages provoke, clarify, comfort, cajole, prioritize and synchronize the day at hand. Do not overthink Morning Pages: just put three pages of anything on the page... and then do three more pages tomorrow" (Cameron, "Morning Pages").

Of course, there are many ways to talk yourself out of doing this: "I have enough trouble getting up in the morning;" "I have to get three kids and myself ready for the day;" "I don't like writing in longhand." The list is nearly endless. I've heard most of them. I've said most of them. But the reality is that I've done Morning Pages on and off since I first read her book in 2003.

The Leadership Yoga Workshop first showed up in my Morning Pages, as did several other popular workshops. They can make a difference for leaders. They not only help you understand what you are really concerned about, but help you discover solutions.

When I decided to apply for the biggest job of my career, which meant leaving a truly great leadership position, the first thing I did was restart my lagging Morning Pages practice. That was almost nine years ago and I'm still an avid practitioner. The routine keeps me grounded, focuses my attention on myself and others, and, I have no doubt, helps me be more successful in anything I decide to pursue.

If Morning Pages just don't work for you, let it go. However, I do encourage you to find some way to regularly create time and space for "self-reflection and thoughtfulness." Goleman is absolutely correct when he identifies this as an important practice for self-awareness and developing emotional awareness.

Practice 3

Setting Your Intention

I wandered my way through college with no clue what I wanted to do after graduation. Luckily for me, I found a degree that seemed to have been designed with my interests in mind. The Bachelor of Arts in Letters at the University of Oklahoma (OU) required that I study history, literature, philosophy, and languages. I loved it! Having a plan for my study meant I graduated in four years. But then what? It no longer says so, but the university catalog at the time indicated that a degree in Letters was considered a pre-law degree.

Even now, for many Letters majors, law school is a common option. And I chose that route. Unlike my undergraduate years, I soon found that I did not love my law school experience. Okay, that's an understatement. I was miserable during my first year, but I didn't drop out because I still didn't know what else I might pursue as a career.

Luckily for me, the Director of Housing at OU, where I had been a Resident Advisor, recommended that I meet his counterpart at Texas Tech University where I was attending law school. I did as he suggested. The Tech Director of Housing lived up to his reputation as a legend in the field. He was gracious and kind and most compelling when he said, "You won't have time to do anything except your law studies this first year, but in the second year, if you'd like a job, come and see us." There's more to this journey of course, but nine months later, I did go see the staff in Housing and ended up with a part-time job as a hall director the following year.

I spent the summer as a law clerk in a small branch of a large law firm where I definitively confirmed that law wasn't the field I wanted to entertain. As the summer wrapped up and I returned to campus, I was miserable at the prospect of returning to law school. Conversely, I found myself thoroughly enjoying my orientation sessions at my new job which, of course, is when I had the epiphany that was to set me on my career path. It finally occurred to me that there were many, many jobs on campus that I would both enjoy and be able to do.

By the time I began my second year of law school, I had an answer to the question I had been asking for four years. I knew what I wanted to do. For the next two years, my goals were simple: survive law school and learn everything I could from my part-time job. Because after those two years, I knew I was going to find work at a college or university, probably in the field of Student Affairs. I didn't yet know what the specific job might be or where I might end up, but I did know I wanted to work on campus. I had a plan, a goal, a sense of purpose and intention.

I learned then that having an intention, a focus for what I was doing each day, helped me through the tough spots. It gave me something bigger than graduation to work toward. It provided context for day-to-day tasks and meaning for my work. Having something other than law school in my life helped me regain my balance, but it was more than that. Knowing why I had chosen to be there, what I wanted to accomplish in that part-time job meant every part of the work taught me something and was therefore worthwhile. Even the getting up in the middle of the night to deal with false fire alarms had something to teach me. My purpose, my intention for the work, gave depth and meaning to the experience far beyond the details of the job.

Setting an Intention

Different yoga teachers mean different things when using the phrase "set an intention." In some cases, it is something similar to a mantra, a word or phrase students are asked to repeat or focus on throughout the class. I'm asking something different of students when I use it, as do many other teachers. Once you get past the circular definitions — *intention* is what one intends while *intent* is a clearly formulated or planned intention — the Merriam-Webster dictionary online gives us a second definition that is more helpful and more in line with the way I use intention in class. That second definition is "a determination to act in a certain way."

For me, taking a moment or two to "set an intention" as we begin a yoga session is about directing our focus during that session. It is part of making the shift in your attention from everything outside of class to the present moment of class time. The focus on your breath and on your current state of being as well as the act of deciding to experience the class in a particular way, are all part of making this shift. It is one reason why the experience of a yoga class is different from other types of exercise classes.

Over time and with repetition, these three practices — focusing on our breath, paying attention, and setting an intention — support our ability to step away from the stresses and noise of our daily routine and drop into the quiet, more deliberate pace for the exercise of yoga. Even a class with music and strenuous movement work is a different type of sound and energy than our day-to-day patterns.

Setting an intention at the start of class is a way to decide, or to use the dictionary term, *determine* what you want or need to focus on during class. It could be as simple as deciding to focus on your breath throughout class. This is a common practice, especially for beginning students. And while it's a simple idea, it can be a surprisingly challenging discipline.

Conversely, setting an intention can be as complicated as deciding that you want to push yourself physically, in which case, you would try poses you might have skipped in the past or go deeper into a pose than you have before. This is complex because it asks the student to stretch their practice while concurrently maintaining a level of awareness of their abilities and limitations.

Setting an intention can also be about your mental or emotional state. In this case, you might decide to hold peace in your heart as you go through the poses. It could be that you want to focus on the way each pose makes you feel physically or emotionally. Some students set the same intention for multiple classes because it is an idea they want to instill in themselves. Often, the circumstances of the day will be such that you need to create an intention to step away from the hustle; other times, you may want your yoga practice to support the emotional work you have been doing. Sometimes the teacher will make a suggestion because the class is designed to focus on a particular aspect of practice. But it's always an individual decision and your choice for an intention can and should change over time.

Setting an intention adds depth and meaning to the physical experience of the class, but it's also common for teachers to end classes by suggesting intentions for the rest of the day. Such intentions are merely recommendations to cultivate the feelings of peaceful energy created during class. These charges or assignments are meant as reminders that we can find peace and calm anywhere; the lessons of yoga are far-reaching.

Intentional Leadership

As leaders, we must examine the available methods for setting intentions and find the one that best suits us. I suspect you already practice some of the approaches, though perhaps you don't think about it this way. A daily to-do list is a way of clarifying what is important to work on during the next few hours. What is an agenda but setting an intention for what you want to focus on or accomplish during a meeting? But the concept of intention for a meeting can extend beyond an agenda. You can set an intention for your behavior in the meeting; you can set an intention around the kind of discussion you want to have.

One possibility is to set an intention to design a meeting which allows participants to be creative. Don't just have a brainstorming session; think about how you need to behave and what you need to say and do as a leader to make it possible for people to know that it is okay to be creative.

What can we do that rewards and supports creative thinking in a meeting? What do we do – purposefully or inadvertently – that shuts it down? In other words, we are setting an intention both for what we want to accomplish and for the actions necessary to make sure we achieve that ideal.

Another possibility for leaders is to set an intention regarding our behavior. Leaders can strive to listen more or to create a space where other voices feel welcomed to speak. They can aim to be open to criticism or new ideas or to keep calm during difficult conversations. There are countless ways a leader can practice setting an intention.

When leaders take time before a meeting to identify what they want or need to accomplish and then set an intention for their behaviors in support of that purpose, they create meetings people value rather than avoid. They also foster an atmosphere within organizations where people feel free to voice their best ideas and their most thoughtful objections because they know it's worth their time and energy.

You can practice setting an intention for large meetings, one-on-one conversations, and events and programs. Taking time to visualize the desired goals for a specific program or envision what you want to achieve when you make a speech are compelling examples of setting intentions. By approaching everything in life with focused intention, you can act in alignment with your values and deepen your leadership work.

Of course, the art of intention is not one solely practiced by individuals. Striving to find a goal is just as vital for organizations. In this arena, we call this activity developing a mission and a vision. Mission and vision statements help organizations define what is important and subsequently focus their attention on that rather than only the day-to-day distractions of accomplishing tasks. In the middle of even ordinary chaos, when there are multiple options and difficult choices to make, well-drafted vision and mission statements guide our decisions. Well-thought-out statements of direction and a clear understanding of organizational values add purpose to what might otherwise be a random set of actions and conclusions. They support making good decisions in difficult situations.

In the same way, well-thought-out values statements act as guides that determine how we collaborate, treat one another, and organize work in accordance with what is important. Leaders who talk about organizational values, missions, and visions in addition to metrics for success set an intention. Leaders who speak about and act in accord with these ideals model the way and set a standard.

In a yoga class, instructors may remind you of the intention set for the class or ask you to notice how you are doing in living your intention. They do this because holding an intention in class is a discipline. It's something we learn to do. It is something that takes practice, application, and willpower because it's often easy to let go and mindlessly go through the postures. When we forget ourselves and our intentions, we miss the opportunities for a deeper experience.

The same challenge is present in our leadership work. It's easier to just get the work done, to focus on the metrics. But we miss the opportunity for sustained leadership if we forget about our reasons to serve and the purposes and values of our organizations. Just as in class, this is a learned behavior. It takes time, discipline, and a steady resolve. Setting intentions at the organizational and personal levels creates touchstones that allow you to grasp what's important even when things don't go well. It's a skill that supports leadership at every level.

Making Choices

The idea of setting an intention can make some people uncomfortable. After all, if we stop to choose a focus, purpose, or style for our actions, it means we have a choice in how we act and react. Actually, we always have a choice in how we react; it's just easier to pretend we don't. There will always be emergencies and priorities and tasks that have to be done right *now!* But not every task is a priority. Not every new idea is urgent. Everything doesn't have to be done immediately. When we have a choice — something we have more often than we like to admit — we can use these three yoga practices of breath, self-awareness, and intention to choose how we respond to the world around us.

When you walk into a yoga studio, it's apparent that it's not your usual exercise class. The studio is devoid of loud, pounding music, pulsing lights, and a peppy instructor trying to rev you up. It's quiet. If music is playing, it's calming, ambient even. There may be candles burning or the scent of weak incense might waft through the air. Students take off their shoes as they step into the room, and then talk quietly or get situated on their yoga mats. Different purposes, different styles. Walking into either a gym or a yoga studio, it is clear their purposes vary and the expectations are dissimilar; therefore, the experiences should be different. A choice has been made and students can choose how they respond to that decision.

As you plan for a meeting, large or small, take some time to think about your purpose. Does it need to be fast-paced and high-energy? This up-tempo version of gathering people is often our default, especially for large meetings. But what would happen if we changed that norm and created an opportunity for people to be reflective and thoughtful together? We don't usually light candles in our work spaces, but there are ways to create harmonious environments that invite people to interact in respectful and productive interactions. But to create such climates, you have to be clear about your purpose and directly express that to the participants. This is another version of setting an intention — being deliberate about what we want to happen and working to create supporting environments.

As leaders, it is our responsibility to take the time to think about our purposes, our intentions. Some of these are personal and therefore private. Other times, they should be shared with colleagues and stakeholders. Our ability to be clear about our intentions improves our ability to engage in the work we have undertaken. As leaders we have a responsibility to engage others effectively and safely in our shared work. A communal intention as described in our mission and vision statements invites others to join us.

A leader's clarity of intention helps make the work safe for everyone. Setting an intention is an important step in creating a good day, but also in establishing effective leadership.

Questions for Reflection

❀ How do you practice setting an intention?

❀ You may call it by different names, but when and how do you take time to determine what is most important for you to accomplish during the day?

❀ When and how do you set an intention for meetings, programs, and conversations?

❀ When and how do you set intentions for your organization? What about for your own leadership?

❀ If you decide that you don't do this regularly, why not? What can you do to create a practice for setting an intention for yourself, for your leadership, and for your organization?

Intention Practices

Setting an Intention for Your Tasks

Planner systems, apps, and calendars all promise to get you organized. Everyone must discover how best to establish an intention. The following three practices are the methods I've found that work for me:

1. **Create a weekly project to-do list on Sunday night.** What are the big-bucket items that really need to be completed at some point during the week? List no more than ten.

2. **Keep a master to-do list.** I've experimented with apps and systems, but what ultimately works best for me is a simple spreadsheet that can be sorted on multiple columns. Each entry includes spaces for the date it was added to the list, a due date (sometimes a real due date, sometimes a speculative one), a completion date, a short description of the task itself, and a column detailing notes that includes all sorts of information or none at all. Each morning, I sort out what's been done and move those entries to a completed tab, then I categorize based on due date which becomes my list for the day. These more detailed items and dates should connect to the weekly to-do list. This one makes some people stressed, but it's the only way I can juggle lost of "balls" and projects and feel confident I haven't lost something along the way.

3. **Create a general calendar.** I'll admit to being a bit silly in the way I do this one. Most people pick one or the other, but I keep both an electronic calendar and a paper calendar. The electronic calendar travels with me on my phone and, since I share it with my husband, we each have an idea about what's going on in the other's day. The paper calendar is where I think. I use a system that lets me easily add, remove, and reorganize pages. I write my Morning Pages in one section. I have a weekly calendar that includes added notes that I use as part-bullet journal, part-daily journal, and part-commonplace book. I keep track of my exercise, my books read for the year, any larger goals I'm working on personal or professional, favorite quotes, poems, and on the odd occasion, tiny bits of art. Some weeks and months are filled to overflowing; others are sparse. However, it's where I can collect and eventually rediscover anything that catches my attention.

It takes less time to do this than to write about it and it expands and contracts depending on my needs. I use it to remind me of my short, mid, and long-term intentions.

Your exercise here is to examine what you are doing to manage your tasks and keep, revise, or change as necessary. Read about the different systems others use and mix and match until you find the right combination for you. I often recommend David Allen's *Getting Things Done*. I don't use his system in its entirety, but some components kept me from feeling completely overwhelmed while still working on campus. Even more, it instilled in me new ways to think about getting my work accomplished.

Setting Daily Intentions

What is your intention for the day? And how will you remind yourself to come back to it in the middle of a hectic schedule?

Unlike the ever-changing tasks on our to-do lists, what is most important may not change often. What are the big ideas that you want to have as the foundation for your leadership today? How do you want to lead? How do you want to be remembered? Big intentions, indeed.

However, it can be difficult to keep those big intentions at the forefront when a day or week is particularly chaotic. On those days, it helps to know that those big ideas are the underpinnings of all we do. In one of those difficult weeks, it can help to shift your focus to accomplishing one or two essential tasks.

My challenge to you when you foresee that sort of day is to set an intention for yourself and your wellbeing. What are you going to do to take care of yourself as you take care of others? Maybe it's paying attention to your breath and your body. Perhaps it's about making time for communication, sharing responsibilities, and asking for help. The list of possibilities is limited only by your understanding of what will be best for you and what will enable you to work in a way that is aligned with your values and highest goals.

Movement

In our metaphorical yoga class, it is time to move past preparation and centering to address movement. Some classes are based on a specific philosophy or design. Kundalini yoga and hot yoga (a specific sequence of *asana*s done in a hot studio) are the immediate examples I can think of. Some are based in a particular teacher's style, such as Iyengar yoga created by B.K.S. Iyengar.

Others are designed to meet particular purposes like restorative yoga, maternity yoga, or yoga for athletes. In the Leadership Yoga Workshop and throughout this book, we will work through the components of a general type of Hatha yoga class. If you recall, Hatha yoga was developed as a way to physically prepare practitioners for meditation. It is "the development of a unique physical culture which has long recognized that posture, movement, and breath are inextricably connected to mental equanimity" (Carrico, M. et al, p. 18).

No matter what you choose, a well-designed class should comprise of multiple components that merge to become a cohesive whole. Each class should move participants through a complete practice of postures, movements, and breathwork in a way that helps them achieve mental equanimity. It's one of the many reasons the practice of yoga is beneficial as part of a leadership practice.

Now it's time to move into the core practices of self-care.

Practice 4

Developing Your Strength

"Do you ever have to yell at your staff?"

This question came out of the blue one day during a dance lesson of all places. A dance studio is its own self-contained world. People come there for a very specific purpose, to partake in the singular interest of dance. People are there to learn to dance. As a result, they rarely disclose the details of their lives outside of the studio.

I took lessons for quite some time before people discovered I was a vice president at a local university. Unsurprisingly, my dance instructor also had an identity outside of the studio that many would find unusual; he was a sergeant in the Army Reserves. We danced together over a number of years as he came and went during tours of duty. That particular day, he was having trouble reconciling what he knew of me, the title I had, and what he experienced as leadership in the military.

I laughed in response to his question, explaining, "No, I don't have to yell at people." After all, as a vice president, the people I supervised were highly experienced, competent and, for the most part, knew how to behave. Additionally, I'm not a yeller by nature. I did tell him that I have a surprisingly effective *stern face* that proves useful when situations necessitate it.

We were in the middle of a dance lesson, so we didn't have a deeper conversation about the diverse styles of leadership needed for different environments. It is an interesting reminder that in the same way our experiences have led us to different ideas about leadership, they have also taught us differently about strength — and about strength in leadership.

There are so many ways to think about strength. The Merriam-Webster online dictionary lists nine definitions, two of which have sub-definitions. They range from being able to resist force and resisting attack to legal, logical, or moral force, to degree of potency. Often when we think of strength as a physical asset, we perceive it as the ability to lift a great deal of weight or to run faster, jump farther — the superman version of strength. And that's not wrong, but it is a limited understanding of strength which limits our ability to recognize other varieties of prowess. It restricts our ability to understand the practice of yoga as a way to develop strength and power.

We have similar limitations in our understandings of other types of strength, don't we? Our experiences may limit our ability to exercise authority effectively if we have only one idea of what it means to be strong as a leader.

This limitation is part of what led to my dance instructor/army sergeant's question. His experience of strong leadership was based on a particular style and he just couldn't imagine this nice dance-lady behaving in such a way. He was right, of course; I don't behave that way.

I have wondered, however, if my style of leadership would be effective in every environment. Maybe I couldn't cut it as a leader in the military without developing a skill for yelling, but I'd like to believe my stern face would do just as well. My husband, who served four years in the Air Force, assures me that my hard-nosed expression would work quite well — if I had enough brass on my collar.

Whether or not I could command in the military in the same way I have led in the world of higher education, I think it benefits all of us to have a wider, more nuanced understanding of strength than is traditionally the case. Subsequently, yoga can help us with this awareness. When we can draw from a variety of perceptions of strength, we can comprehend leadership — and our world — in a completely different light.

Standing Tall

Throughout these five Core Practice chapters, we will explore simple postures from yoga and discuss what the poses can offer us. Pictures will be included and, of course, there are many yoga classes available online if you wish to explore a pose more thoroughly.

There are several ways to begin a yoga class – seated, standing, or even lying on the floor. For our purposes, we'll begin our exploration of poses through standing poses since these cultivate strength. The first one, the basis for many other poses, is *Tadasana*, translated as Mountain Pose.

Strength is one of the attributes we often ascribe to mountains. When tasks are difficult, we may compare them to climbing a mountain that seems to grow taller each day. It takes strength to climb such mountains. But in yoga, we shift the metaphor from climbing the mountain to being the mountain.

If you were to look into a class practicing *Tadasana*, you would see a group of people standing still, not quite at attention – they aren't rigid like soldiers – but erect, straight and tall. It doesn't look like much, but it is work. Because many of us spend a great deal of our days seated, standing tall in Mountain Pose asks us to use muscles in ways and for lengths of time they may be unused to.

Actually moving into *Tadasana* in and of itself is work as it requires you to remain focused and develop balance. In *Tadasana*, we work to keep our feet grounded, solid upon the earth, strong, unmoving, while simultaneously lifting our hearts and heads toward the sky. When we are grounded, we are strong enough to soar. We aren't simply standing; we work to be both still and active, peaceful and strong. A bulwark rather than an obstacle.

All standing poses teach us "to stand on our own two feet." They "invigorate, heat, and strengthen the entire body, increasing our circulation and stamina" (Farhi, p. 87). Mountain Pose, in particular, teaches us that strength isn't always a show of force. It doesn't have to be loud or in your face. True strength is grounded, calm, and ever-present. Practicing *Tadasana* reminds us that we too can have the strength of the mountain.

A Leader's Strength

Outside of yoga, when we use the word posture, we tend to mean the act of standing or sitting upright – good posture – or slumping – poor posture. Joseph Pilates described the importance of posture this way: "[N]ever slouch, as doing so compresses the lungs, overcrowds other vital organs, rounds the back, and throws you off balance." His use of the phrase "throws you off balance" is literal, but concurrently works metaphorically. After all, changing from a slump to standing tall actually can help change your mood and your sense of self.

I think most of us have experienced that moment of taking a deep breath, squaring our shoulders, and lengthening (though we usually call it straightening or stiffening) our spine before doing something we find challenging or that makes us nervous. That moment spent on our posture actually does help.

Conversely, there's the not-so-positive use of the word, though usually we shift it to the gerund form – posturing. Generally, this calls for a *Wizard-of-Oz*-moment where we are to be convinced to pay no attention to the "man behind the curtain." If someone doesn't have the ability to do what needs to be done, they might posture, pose, bluster, or make sure there's a lot of smoke blowing to distract others from the reality. Clearly, a negative connotation. We don't like fakery.

And yet, we often advise people to "fake it until you make it." In such a situation, we don't advocate someone take on a task for which they are unqualified. Usually, this is a way to encourage someone who is experiencing imposter syndrome, of helping someone have the strength to take on a challenging new task or role.

But what if imposter syndrome simply means we are stretching beyond our comfort zone? Instead of feeling we are someplace we shouldn't be, what if we reimagine this experience as trying a new, more difficult posture or way of engaging in our work? When we encourage people to fake it until they make it, we intend it as encouragement as they try a new *posture*, a new way of working, stretching, and growing. We are emboldening them to adopt the posture of confidence until they feel confident. It's not a suggestion that they bluff. It's a fine and significant distinction.

As we consider the leadership lessons to be learned from yoga, it's important to consider this distinction. Yoga and leadership both ask us to try new things, to stretch ourselves, to put ourselves in positions that are uncomfortable. This is one of the times we need to engage our self-awareness.

As we try a new posture in class or take on new responsibilities at work, it's critical that we are honest about our abilities. Are we strong enough to try this new pose? Is our hesitation at taking on a new responsibility a failure of confidence or an honest understanding that we aren't fully prepared to take on this new role? Both practices require us to be self-aware enough to keep from hurting ourselves or others as we stretch and grow. It's a delicate balance and it takes internal strength to pursue something new. Similarly, it takes mental fortitude to conclude something is not right for us at a given time.

Leadership and Power

There's another standing pose I teach during the workshop. It's one of a series of three Warrior Poses. *Virabhadrasana II* is, like *Tadasana*, deceptively simple. From a wide-legged stance, with arms extended, we bend one knee in a 90-degree angle. Envision one hand reaching back toward the past, while the other, the one we look out over, reaching toward the future. Holding the pose with strength and calmness, while breathing slowly and evenly takes practice. Holding the pose for several breaths takes strength in the legs. Being able to extend your arms from your shoulders while staying strong, steady, and relaxed, takes strength. But it is the locating of one's center that makes this pose the most rewarding.

Physically, this means not leaning out over the bent leg or back toward the straight leg; it means not bending forward at the waist or arching the back. The posture challenges us to be both strong and supple. Mentally and emotionally, *Virabhadrasana II* teaches about staying centered in our lives. It encourages us to stand in the present no matter how challenging the present may be. Not yearning for the past or wishing for the future, but standing in the present, facing what is coming toward us, strong and calm.

Leaders need physical stamina, but more importantly, they need the internal strength of a warrior. This internal fortitude is the power that comes from leading from a deep core of values and purpose. When leaders move from a place of service to an organization and the people who are part of that organization, their strength is an asset. Individuals who hold positions of leadership need to understand that they wield power and authority over others. Understanding this reality permits leaders to make positive decisions regarding the use of such responsibilities.

Fearing their power or refusing to use it appropriately is as much a disservice to the members of the organization as abusing one's authority, though it is felt in different ways. Failing to use authority to support the work of an organization's members is an abdication of the leader's responsibility. Perceiving strength in a positive light is integral to leadership.

It is important to realize that warrior strength does not equate to stubborn persistence or petulance. Stubborn persistence has a place – it's part of the way I completed law school – but it's not the only way to accomplish difficult tasks. The battle, if we must use such language, is the internal one. The challenge is developing the ability to be both soft and strong.

Similar to trying a new and difficult yoga pose, the lesson is to persist but not to the point of harming oneself or others. It is possible to work with difficult people *and* to lead through tribulations without becoming a bully or yelling. Becoming a centered, but strong warrior is an achievable goal.

The Warrior and the Mountain both teach us that the opportunity presented to leaders is to experience the moment as it is, not as we wish it to be. They show us how to remain grounded in our values as we strive to live them. Strength is not necessarily force, but being the stable point of calm in the chaos of our world. People who can lead from this point of value-based tranquility have the diligence to do what needs to be done and the ability to take action without causing harm to themselves or others. This is the strength we learn in yoga.

Strength of Character

We make decisions that reflect our ethics, values, and character all day, every day, even if we don't stop to think of them that way. Take something as routine as driving.

When you are late, do you choose to stay within the speed limit and accept the consequences? Or do you choose to speed? If you are stopped and get a ticket, do you accept that as a consequence of your choice or try to get out of it? These are questions of ethics and values for each of us, even if people do violate the speed limit all the time. If we know there is no consequence for speeding, but it is bad for the neighborhood if you race down the street, there are different, more subtle questions to sort out as we decide what speed to drive.

As members of organizations and communities, we face complex questions and make difficult decisions every day. We have faced some so often that our responses are routine, without thought. But what happens when the circumstances change? What happens when you take on the responsibilities of leadership?

Leadership can push us to rethink the choices we make while presenting different questions and issues for us to wrestle with. Being clear about our own ethics and values will help us have the strength to make the best choices we can make in difficult circumstances.

Cultivating Strength

Taking time to breathe and reflect before making a decision helps us make better decisions and have the strength to carry out those decisions even in difficult times.

Paying attention to circumstances, to the effect of the possible decisions, and to our alignment with organizational rules and personal values will help us be strong in the face of disagreement.

Being clear about what is most important in a given situation will help set clear intentions to do the most good and the least harm through our actions and decisions.

Finding ways to be both strong and supple physically, emotionally, and mentally is leadership work.

Question for Reflection

✿ How do you understand the idea of strength in leadership?

Take some time to really explore this question. Think about strong leadership you have seen in the world or experienced in your communities and organizations. What images does the idea of a strong leader bring to mind? Spend time analyzing your understanding of strength in all of its aspects.

✿ What does the idea of strength of character mean to you?

Spend some time reflecting on this quote by Criss Jami, an American poet and essayist: "To share your weakness is to make yourself vulnerable; to make yourself vulnerable is to show your strength." Or perhaps read some of Brené Brown's work on shame.

✿ Where have you seen leaders exhibit what you define as strength of character; where have you seen leaders fail in this area?

✿ How do you understand power?

Strength Practices

Try These Poses

Find a book, video, or class and practice *Tadasana* and *Virabhadrasana.* Experience what these poses have to teach you. Write about it in your Morning Pages or journal.

Strengthen Your Leadership

All leadership positions include some level of power and authority over others. Some leaders abuse this power while others shy away from their responsibilities and, in doing so, fall short of being the fully capable leader the world needs them to be. Do you understand the power you command in your position? How do you exercise the power that comes with your title, the authority you have over others, and the responsibility entrusted to you as a leader?

Be honest with yourself. Are you meeting your obligations with strength and integrity? Are you abusing your authority and power? Are you short-changing yourself and your organization by not using the power that you have as a leader and as a person? Reflect on your understanding of the concepts of strength and power.

Tadasana (Mountain Pose)

We begin with our feet, making certain we are not leaning forward or backward, ensuring we aren't standing on the outsides of our feet, but we're completely centered. Then, we check the alignment of our legs and pelvis which should be neutral. Our back isn't arched nor are our hips tucked in tightly. We are working to make sure our base is secure, that we are fully grounded and steady. Remember, the base of the mountain is wide and strong.

Next, we move our attention to our torso and arms. Many of us have a habit of keeping our shoulders up around our ears, so to rectify that, we roll our shoulder blades down. This lets our arms fall naturally and opens our chest. Think about lifting your heart toward the sky which also helps you open your chest as you focus on making your breathing slow and deep.

Finally, we turn our attention to our head and neck. Think of your neck as being long, but don't work at stretching it. Just lower those shoulders and create space between them and your head. Your chin should be parallel to the floor. Now, imagine there's a small hook at the top of your head with a string attached to it and someone is gently pulling the string up. It's not hurting or forcing anything, just encouraging you to lift the top of your head toward the ceiling. Close your eyes or look down at the floor.

From the grounded support of your legs, let your upper body be light and lift up.

Virbhadrasana II (Warrior II)

We begin *Virbhadrasana II* in Mountain Pose, standing tall and strong and centered over our two feet. From here, we spread our legs four to four and a half feet apart. And we stop to re-center ourself. Often, spreading our legs apart causes us to bend slightly to feel balanced. So, take a moment to make certain you are neither bending forward nor arching your back.

Next, turn your right foot outward 90 degrees and your back heel out 45 degrees. What most people do here is turn their hips and upper

body slightly to the right to accommodate that rotated leg. Stop to ensure your hips are facing forward.

You will probably already be feeling an unfamiliar stretch in your legs and hips. Next, bring your arms up to shoulder height and stretch them parallel to the floor. Bend your right knee until your leg forms a 90-degree angle or as close to it as you can comfortably achieve.

Two important safety factors come into play here. Don't push your knee out past your ankle. You may need to adjust the distance between your feet to find the right stance and you may not be able to get to 90-degrees. No matter the angle of your knee, you want there to be a straight line from your knee to your ankle.

The second safety reminder is to make sure your right knee is not collapsing inwards. If your inner thighs are tight and your knee is not able to be directly over your ankle, adjust your stance to one you can hold with your knee comfortably in the right position. Press your right heel down into the ground (keep your toes relaxed) and press the outside of your left foot toward the ground.

Once your legs are well-positioned, check your stance, making sure your hips are still squared toward the front and your torso tall. Now, look out over the fingertips of your right hand, but don't lean toward that hand. If anything, stretch your left hand back to keep you centered over both legs. Hold the pose for a couple of breaths and gaze forward over your hand, peering toward your future with strength and calmness.

When you are done, straighten your right leg and come back to Mountain Pose. Close your eyes, breathe, and pay attention to your mental and emotional experience, as well as your physical experience. When you are ready, repeat on the left side.

Practice 5

Understanding Balance

I've lost track of how many times over the course of my career I've been asked about work-life balance or been invited to participate in a panel discussion on the topic. The articles I've read on the subject are literally countless. Over time though, I quit talking about work-life balance and began focusing on something more doable: living an integrated life.

I'm a word nerd who is fascinated by etymology and intrigued by their multiple uses in our language. While I don't actually read the dictionary, I turn to it often. Looking up balance, I found that it has two primary definitions as a noun, both of which are relevant to this topic. The two definitions are: "An even distribution of weight enabling someone or something to remain upright and steady" and "a condition in which different elements are equal or in the correct proportions" (*Lexico.com*).

When people ask me about work-life balance, I think they are using the second definition. They seem to be asking how to get the two elements of work and life balanced in some ideal of equal proportions. Or perhaps they are asking what the correct proportions should be. I don't answer either question because they are too subjective. More importantly, I think they are asking the wrong question.

Asking about work-life balance assumes there are only two aspects to this equation – work and life – that sit on opposite ends of a scale, and once we get them into alignment, all is well. Even the people asking the question know it's not that simple. Going to a professional conference where you see friends you have known for 20 years, where you will eat out, sightsee, attend professional development sessions, and be exhausted when you get home at the end of a succession of very long days – what side of the scale does that go on? Does it go on a different side if you bring your family with you? Does it go on the opposite side if you refuse to sightsee? Clearly the concept of work-life balance is more complex and depends on more than just balancing two elements of your life.

Eventually, a few years into my career, and after trying to face the dilemma a number of times, I changed the question – how does one live an integrated life, a life in which responsibilities in all roles are interwoven into something more complicated and complete as life ebbs and flows? For me, this became a values-based question.

Day by day, week by week, semester by semester, I have tried to make the best decisions I can based on what is most important to me. Sometimes, family takes precedence over work, but that doesn't mean I stop going to work. Sometimes one part of a family needs more attention than other family members. Other times, such as the opening week of a semester or during an emergency on campus, I would say to my husband, "I'll see you in a week," since I knew I would come home late and tired every night for seven or eight days in a row.

I've always taken my vacation each summer and at various other times as well. It's not a badge of honor to never use your vacation. Nor is a badge of honor to save all your sick days. They are there for a reason, so I stay home when I'm sick. On vacations, I make my best effort to disconnect, though my success varies depending on my job and the circumstances.

While I might not have been able to fully disconnect, my effort resulted in more effective time management. Do I live a balanced life all the time? Of course not. But because I work to make deliberate choices and to keep what's important to me in the mix, I do better than I would have otherwise.

My version of how I spent my time might not work for anyone else. It's not supposed to. Living an integrated life is a subjective concept, not a one-size-fits-all type of revelation. I try to make the best decisions I can in line with my values, my sense of what is most important at any given time. I don't always get it right, but over the course of my career, I've found the right combination for me.

Pushing and Pulling

Yoga teaches us about that other definition of balance. In class, we practice poses that are considered balance poses. Balance poses ask us to find a way to evenly distribute our weight to allow us to remain upright and steady. Yoga teacher and author Eric Schiffmann puts it this way: "A proper balance is necessary between push and yield. Too much push has a driven quality that betrays a harshness and severity toward oneself." Conversely, he writes, "Yoga done in too yielding a fashion never develops the openings or strength that provide the energized relaxation this is so appealing and revitalizing" (p. 51).

During yoga teacher training sessions, our instructor Charles gave us a fascinating demonstration of this idea. He stood and extended one arm out from his shoulder. The game was to see how long it took for one of us to bend his arm at the elbow. In the first round, Charles exerted full effort to keep his arm straight. His entire body was rigid with the effort. A student volunteered to try and managed it fairly quickly. It took a bit of *oomph*, but it wasn't terribly difficult for her.

Then Charles tried it a different way. He once again extended his arm to its full length perpendicular to his body, but this time, he relaxed the rest of his body. His breath was slow and calm. Instead of using brute strength and rigidity, his posture and mental state were relaxed and calm. You can guess what happened. The same student tried to bend his arm but couldn't. Neither could the next two students who tried. The point was clear; effort and inflexibility were not as successful as resilient softness.

You might expect that we watched this demonstration while discussing strength, but it was during our lessons regarding balance poses. Often, when we begin trying balance poses, our natural reaction is to stiffen up as we try to hold the pose. We act as if balance is achieved by taking a rigid, unyielding stance; we try to push our way into balance. Charles' lesson was to show us another way.

Instead of muscling our way into balance, we might do better to achieve our goal through flexibility and tranquility. Being soft, supple, able to move as we work to find our balance point, is a better way to practice yoga. It's also a better way to find balance in our life and leadership.

It was Schiffman who said, "Yoga that has a proper balance between active and passive feels wonderful. It is not overly aggressive or torpid, but a harmonious blend of push and yield. It is at once both vigorous and quiet, like a perfectly centered top spinning so fast it appears motionless" (p. 51-52). In the same way, one of the challenges of living an integrated life is finding our own still point between pushing to get things done and understanding that there are times we have to wait for things to happen. We must discover ways to be strong, rather than unyielding while all the while learning when to push, to pull, or to do neither. All of these statements are equally applicable to our practice of leadership.

Finding balance between being decisive and listening to others takes time and experience. Standing strong and being able and willing to change one's mind is a balancing act. Leading the way and inviting others into leadership are equally important. Ultimately, finding the appropriate mix is both challenging and possible.

Lessons from a Tree

In the Leadership Yoga Workshop, the balance posture I teach is the deceptively simple Tree Pose, *Vrksasana*. Most people have seen it – a person standing on one leg, with the other foot pressed firmly on the inside thigh of the standing leg, arms stretched overhead, palms pressed together. It looks motionless in pictures.

It turns out that we don't even have to do the entire pose to experience its lessons. All we have to do is stand on one foot. First, take your shoes off. Now, standing barefoot, lift one foot up just to your ankle. Breathe slowly and shift your attention to the standing foot. Notice how the muscles in your foot and the tendons in your ankle are moving, shifting ever so slightly to support you. Your body adjusts as you inhale and exhale and your foot makes tiny alterations in response. And you begin to realize that balance is not static. It's certainly not rigid or still. It is supple and open. Maintaining balance requires movement. It requires us to change in response to circumstances.

Vrksasana teaches us about balance, strength, and centering ourselves. But the richness of Tree Pose comes when we attempt the full pose. It's awkward. It even feels a bit unsafe to stand on one foot and lift the other high on your leg. It's counterintuitive since to achieve balance in this pose, we have to move our weight off-center.

In other poses, we shift our weight even more significantly. The idea of being off-center on our way to finding our balance causes some people to tense up. Arms are flailing, legs wiggling. People stick their tushes out or tuck them in tightly all in a frantic effort to keep that foot off the ground. And yet, a simple lesson of *Vrksasana* is that when you start falling out of the pose, just put your foot down. It's as simple as that.

Stop trying so hard to be balanced. It doesn't hurt to put your foot to the ground or touch a nearby wall if you need to. Put your foot down, stand tall, take a deep breath. Try again – just like life and leadership. We fall out of balance all the time and we always will.

Let's stop flailing around and come back to what's most important to us. Take a deep breath. Try again.

Falling Forward

Apparently, walking is merely falling forward and catching ourselves again and again. If you Google "walking is falling," there are numerous articles available of varying levels of complexity from a variety of exercise sciences. The simplest explanation I found was by a group called Core Walking. Their website explains the concept like this: "The way it works is pretty simple – moving through space with one foot in front of the other, as my legs switch there is a moment when the upper body is forward of the front leg. In that moment, the brain registers that the body is about to fall and the brain tells the psoas major to initiate the pull of the back leg forward to prevent a crash."

This means we are quite literally falling all of the time. I find that oddly reassuring because mostly, I don't end up on the floor (though I have done my share of falling through the years). I was extraordinarily good at falling down the stairs in our home during my pre-teen years. I have a couple of mildly embarrassing stories like walking to class as a college freshman, stepping off a perfectly normal curb, and falling full-length into the street for no apparent reason or sliding down a short flight of stairs on my shins a month into a new job. I have a spectacular story of doing some sort of flip into the air and landing flat on my back between rows of seats in my high school auditorium. Clearly, there were times when I was better at falling than walking. But, like most of us, my feet and brain coordinate well enough that I don't have to think about what an amazing balancing act simply walking is.

Yoga teacher and author Gary Kraftsow writes, "When we are standing the bodily base of support is our feet; when we are seated, the base is the buttocks and legs; and when we are lying down the base is the full length of our body. In general, the larger the base, the greater the stability" (p. 114). Balance poses force us to practice balance on a very small base – one foot. But then we remember walking, moving from one small base to the next. I think in our seemingly never-ending quest for balance, we forget we are actually quite good at this balancing act, all things considered.

If we spent our lives seated in one place, we might feel balanced. Simple enough. But we aren't usually satisfied with that idea. We get up and move. We try new things and challenge ourselves. In other words, we shift from stability and balance to imbalance on purpose. I think this is an interesting way to reframe the idea of balance. We don't really want stasis, though sometimes in a hectic world that feels like a good idea. One of the reasons this is such a complex equation is that we choose to change our circumstances, we keep moving, so we keep falling forward.

Perhaps we aren't really looking for balance. Possibly, instead, we are like the baby learning to walk, constantly testing this balance-thing as we attempt to explore our world. Learning to move in new ways is amazing when it works and a bit painful when it doesn't. Like the toddler, we run into things. Sometimes, we can't get to what we want when we want it, and yes, we lose our balance and fall. But each time we try something new, we learn something. We develop new skills, new muscles, and new ways of responding to the world around us. And to get to that new place, achieve that new skill, or take on a new responsibility, we have to go through a period of imbalance and instability.

I wonder how our perceptions about those moments when we long for work-life balance would change if we understood the idea of balance this way. When we feel out-of-balance, it means we have moved off-center or have been moved away from stability; we must change something – move that back foot forward to catch ourselves.

What if life is, in fact, a series of moments of imbalance followed by balance each day, and every day, as we move, we are falling forward into something new? If that's the case, then being off-balance is, in fact, a normal state. That's not necessarily a comfortable reality. Sometimes it's even painful and we bump our noses or give our heads a wallop as I did that day in the high school auditorium. Then the recovery time takes a bit longer, but recover we do. We try again to move forward and find a new form of balance.

In this view, when we are in the middle of significant change, we are in liminal space – that uncomfortable spot between the old and the not-yet-realized new. It's that space between the first step and the one yet to come. We don't know yet if we'll be coordinated, fall, step on a rock, or move smoothly onto solid ground. But we move forward anyway, trusting that we are actually pretty good at this falling-forward activity and that we'll figure it out as we go.

Balanced Leadership

In our leadership, we add an additional element to this idea of staying balanced. In the work environment, we are forced to collaborate with others who have their own ideas about balance, their own values, and their own sense of what is important. Therefore, this difficult balancing act, this idea of living an integrated life as a leader, becomes infinitely more complex.

The practice of partner yoga has something to teach us about balanced leadership. The authors of *Partner Yoga: Making Contact for Physical, Emotional, and Spiritual Growth* explain such an act of equilibrium as the following: "Each partner must first find (their) own balance, bringing balance into the partnership. The pose is based upon mutual support, not one partner holding the other up" (Carrol, C. & L. Kimata, p. 133). I think this idea is particularly important for leadership.

In partner yoga and leadership, we have to stand on our own two feet and trust the other person to do the same. Partner work and leadership require interpersonal communication and a respect of abilities and boundaries. In other words, both require honest communication. For leadership and partner yoga to work, everyone involved needs to be clear about personal and organizational priorities and values.

Done well, a partner's support provides a level of safety and a counterbalance that allows each person to let go of anything that is holding them back. In yoga, a partner can help us deepen our stretch and gain more benefit from a pose. In leadership, working effectively with partners helps everyone achieve their goals. And when it all works, it's fun.

Even in a short interaction in a class with a person who is a relative stranger, what comes after the initial discomfort is a sense of play and confidence that permits each person to further explore their limitations. People laugh together and soften into the poses. It can be just as true in our organizational work. Once we begin to work together and develop the beginnings of familiarity and trust, even the most difficult task becomes more enjoyable and the results more interesting. It creates a positive feedback loop as each success leads to the next.

Partner yoga reminds us we aren't really experiencing balance if my experience comes at your expense. Balanced leadership matters for us all. Balance poses remind us that leading integrated lives or exercising effectively balanced leadership takes continuous awareness. They both require us to pay attention to ourselves and to the people around us, to honor our commitments, be honest with ourselves and others, and to make adjustments as necessary.

The practice of understanding balance truly comes when we are willing and able to shift in response to changing circumstances, when we are strong enough to support our own weight, and when we are willing to reach out for help or touch a foot to the ground when needed.

Questions for Reflection

❀   What is most important to you?

To live an integrated life and to practice balanced leadership, it's important to have a clear understanding of our own most deeply held values. There are many different value clarification exercises available. Find one or two and go through the exercise. You might be surprised, especially if you have experienced a major life change or it has been several years since you spent some time thinking about what is important to you.

❀   How are you feeling right now?

Take some time to evaluate your current status. If you are feeling stressed, anxious, or burned-out, can you identify the reasons for your feelings? Once you have done that, honestly identify which of these causes are outside of your control and which are within your control. Be honest with yourself. Sometimes we act as if things are outside of our control, but when we stop and really do the analysis, we realize we have taken on stressors, extra work, or other things that no one really expected us to do. Other times we try to change things that aren't ours to control. Are you pushing when you should be yielding or vice versa?

❀ Is this just one of those times?

There are times when life is really out of balance. To higher education professionals who are considering going back to school for a doctorate, I tell them that life won't be in balance for that time period. The same is true if you have a new baby in the family, a loved one who is seriously ill, or a family member who needs elder care. There will be things you have to give up.

For some people, it's movies, time with friends, or Netflix. For others, it's sleep or a clean house. Part of feeling out of balance may be your expectations of yourself or others. If this is "one of those times," what can you let go of?

❀ What expectations can you set aside? What conversations need to happen with colleagues or friends?

❀ What is truly essential and what's important but not necessary right now?

Balance Practices

Practice a Balance Pose

Physically, balance is an important element of continuing health and wellbeing, especially as we age. Practice Tree Pose regularly. Or if that's a bit too advanced, find times during the day to stand on one foot, then the other for 30 seconds. Try it with your eyes closed. Work to increase the time you do this as your legs strengthen and your balance improves.

Calendar/Time Review

Make a list of the things that you say you value or that are important to you. Take a look at your calendar, or if you only keep scheduled appointments on your calendar, take time over the next week to keep track of everything you spend time on. Then sit down and compare the list and the calendar. The calendar/time review often tells us some hard truths about the choices we make.

We say health is important, but never find time to do anything that supports our physical health.

We say learning is important, but make no time for reading, taking a course, or practicing something new.

We say family is important, but we take on more at work.

When work is hectic and we may have to put in more hours, what are we doing to explain that to family and friends? Are we finding different ways to support them? Where are we touching a foot to the ground or asking for help from colleagues, family, or friends? And if we aren't asking for help, why not?

Add to your analysis your insights about the items that are causing stress and anxiety. Of the items that are in your control, what changes can you make to bring your actions more in line with your values and priorities?

Of the areas you can't change, what can you do to balance them with activities you find restorative?

What knowledge and understanding can you bring together to create a more integrated, a more balanced life for yourself?

Vrksasana (Tree Pose)

As with all standing poses, begin in Mountain Pose. Take time to bring your body into alignment, ground your legs and lift your torso. Enjoy the feeling of standing tall.

Now, shift your weight onto your left leg, remembering not to accommodate by moving your hip to the side. It's still a strong, straight leg, but you have more weight on the left leg than on the right. Find a spot on the wall in front of you or on the floor about six feet in front of you. If you feel more comfortable with the idea of support, you can stand by a wall, but keep in mind you can always touch your foot to the ground.

Lift your right foot slightly off the ground and position it alongside your ankle. Ensure that your toes are on the ground and that your heel is resting lightly on your ankle. Open your right leg to the side.

Bring your hands palm-to-palm at the center of your chest and take a deep breath. Exhale fully and, on your next breath, slide your foot up along your leg. Stop at whatever point is comfortable. But please don't use the little notch at your knee as a place for your heel to rest. It's possible to hurt yourself by pushing on the knee joint there. Bring your foot just below the knee or, if you can, above your knee.

When you find a point of relative stability, stay there, breathing slowly. Or slowly lift your arms overhead while keeping your palms together. You're in tree pose. When you are ready, bring your right foot to the ground, stand in Mountain Pose, and breathe. Do the same thing on the other leg.

Don't be surprised if you have two different experiences. The way we use our muscles can routinely affect this pose. One side might be stronger or weaker, groin muscles might be tighter or more relaxed. The second attempt may feel more familiar now that you've accomplished one version. Don't worry about the differences. Be aware of them and be gentle with yourself as you try the poses. Learn what a tree has to teach you.

Practice 6

Stretching Yourself

In this chapter, we explore the principal idea that led to the creation of the Leadership Yoga Workshop, thanks to Larraine Matusak's aforementioned book. "Stretch" is one of the words shared between yoga and leadership. Matusak is equally clear about two points.

First, we all have the potential to be leaders; secondly, everyone, even someone who naturally gravitates toward leadership, has skills to develop and lessons to learn on their way to effective leadership. In other words, we have to change and grow. We have to risk trying new ideas or new ways of behaving. We have to stretch. We have to risk being uncomfortable as we move into the unknown.

As leaders, we ask people to come on this journey into the unknown with us. We ask them to trust us enough to take a risk and to be uncomfortable with us. Sometimes we push them into new responsibilities that causes them stress or discomfort. The Leadership Yoga Workshop invites participants to experience that stretch literally and to remember what it feels like to try something new. To feel awkward and unsure. To be a beginner again.

Leadership and yoga both ask us to stretch not only our muscles and our skills, of course, but our awareness of ourselves and the world around us. Both practices ask us to push ourselves. Yoga teaches us to push gently while listening to our bodies as we work to stretch into new postures or relax more deeply into familiar ones. Leadership work challenges us to spur ourselves, our colleagues, and our organizations and communities into new ways of thinking without causing harm.

As a new vice president at Trinity University, I was asked by a new colleague, "What is your tolerance for risk?" I had never thought about it that way before and so didn't have a good answer. Even now, I'm not sure I do.

What I do know is that over time, I have learned to be more comfortable with uncertainty. I have learned to be flexible in trying new things and more aware of my own intuition and experience when making difficult decisions. I have learned how to stretch safely and how to support others as they work to understand their abilities. I highly recommend stretching as part of your yoga, leadership, and life practices.

Habits – Mind and Body

A habit is a behavior that takes little or no conscious thought and therefore frees up the mind to pay attention to other things. Some habits we purposefully create, others just come into existence. A habit about where we put our keys when we enter the house saves us from having to search the house for them the next time we want to leave. Habits in morning routines mean we don't have to think through every decision to get the day started. We work to cultivate habits around positive behaviors.

On the other hand, habitual behaviors can make it difficult to make significant changes because we have to actively work to think about behaving differently.

And then there are the habits that have been with us for so long and are so ingrained that we don't even recognize the behavior as a habit. I certainly didn't understand how many habits of movement or posture I had until I began yoga classes.

Try this for a moment. Reach overhead and clasp your hands with fingers interlaced. Now, keeping your hands clasped together, bring them down in front of you. Look to see how you interlaced your fingers. Right over left or left over right? Let go and lift your hands overhead again. This time, when you clasp your hands together interlace your fingers the opposite way from your norm. In other words, if you normally have right fingers over left, this time try left over right.

What did it feel like to you? Easy or awkward? Most find it at least somewhat awkward. I've watched some people bring their hands down to look and go finger by finger to make the swap, finding that such attention is needed to break the habit. The practice is so ingrained, not only do we not have to think about doing it, it feels *wrong* to do it any other way.

Most of us have similar habits when crossing our arms, stepping up on a curb, or walking up a flight of stairs – we usually begin with the same foot every time. Yoga helped me become aware that when I get into the driver's seat, I often slide in and stay perched on my right hip. Now, I try to remember to shift into a more balanced posture before I start driving.

When we stretch in yoga, one of the reasons it can be difficult is due to our habits. If we spend most of our time seated in a chair, our hamstrings tighten up and bending forward to touch our toes is difficult, sometimes painful, and often impossible. Creating a new habit of getting up, moving around, stretching during the day will help our hamstrings loosen up and allow us to be more flexible.

Our innate need for habits follows us into the workplace and is ever-present in how we work, lead, and think. Sometimes they are our own; sometimes the habits are organizational. You experience organizational habits when a long-term member of an organization tells a newer member, "That's not how we do it here." This can be an important cultural reminder, but can also be evidence of behavior and thinking that could use some stretching. And that stretch is every bit as uncomfortable as leaving our desk to touch our toes.

When I joined Trinity University, my predecessor had been in the position for 20 years or so. A year and a half into my tenure, a colleague, who had worked with my predecessor for most of those years, told me he was still adjusting to having a new supervisor. It wasn't that he didn't like to try new things or that he thought what I was asking was unreasonable; it was simply that he had to think about things now, explaining, "When we did (x program), all I had to do was pull out the relevant folder, change some dates, and then do what we did last year." It worked and had become so routine he had stopped asking himself to stretch. Now, here I was asking different questions, suggesting changes, and disrupting long-established norms. I was bumping into habits.

Trying something new does take more thought, often more time, and may or may not work. Trying something new asks us to stretch.

What It Takes to Stretch

I suspect when people who have never tried yoga think about it, they imagine yogis standing on their heads or seated in Lotus position or perhaps twisted into positions that don't seem anatomically possible. People who say they can't do yoga often think they aren't flexible enough or that they couldn't possibly move their bodies in the ways yoga must require. The reality though is that yoga supports everyone becoming more flexible. Like everything else, in yoga we start where we are and learn, grow, and stretch as we practice.

Let's consider the forward bend *Uttanasana*, a relatively simple pose that is actually very challenging for many people. If the only measure of success is whether or not you can touch your toes, some people will never achieve success. However, when we pay attention to our alignment and use our breath to support us, everyone has the ability to learn to bend forward further than when we first tried the pose. Success in this pose is learning how to stretch a bit further.

Some of the reasons people struggle with the forward bend are due to physical characteristics such as tight hamstring muscles and hip flexors. These are areas that take time and patience to adjust. But body mechanics and movements also determine the depth of our forward bend.

If we understand a forward bend as simply rounding over to reach our toes, even the most limber person will face some challenges. On the other hand, if we understand that our hips function as a large hinge and move from our hip joint, the posture and our experience with it will be completely different. Not any simpler, but ultimately deeper and more effective. The way we stand, our alignment, influences our ability to stretch physically.

In addition to understanding some of the mechanics of movement, it's important to remember the importance of paying attention. If you recall, we discussed pushing and pulling as we try new things. Being constantly stretched isn't good for our muscles or our mental and emotional states. When we use the phrase "being stretched thin," we acknowledge it is inherently an unhealthy way to live. Pushing too hard to stretch is a sure way to hurt oneself in a yoga class. And so, in yoga classes, we support our efforts to stretch by also spending time in postures that teach us to contract, to pull inward.

I'm always intrigued by the dynamic of paradoxes such as this – the experience of contracting to encourage proper stretching. The practice of yoga teaches us the importance of both types of movement. In a yoga class, we move into postures that stretch us, and then we reverse the action and pull in. Sometimes we move from a tight pose to an expansive one. The lesson, of course, is that we need both to be healthy. Being in either mode all the time isn't good for us physically, mentally, or emotionally.

Yoga encourages us to practice being more expansive mentally and emotionally, as well as physically. Conversely, many people are over-stretched by all of the competing claims on their time and attention, which would suggest finding ways to pull in even for a short time. The practice of pulling in and contracting supports our ability to stretch in challenging times. Understanding the importance of both stretching and contracting in our physical experience helps us manage our emotions and our energy.

Stretching as a Leader

These same concepts can be applied to leadership in an integral way. Whether facing difficult decisions, trying to manage all of the responsibilities of leadership and personal obligations, or taking care of oneself as you are asked to take care of others, it is important to think about your organizational habits and alignments.

What are the values of your organization and how will your decisions reflect those values? What are your personal values and how are your actions a way of living out those values?

When our actions, our personal values, and our organizational values align, we are better positioned to make difficult decisions. When we take time to breathe and deepen our focus on purpose, we trust the hard decisions we have to make, even if we don't like making them.

Understanding and working with the dynamic pairing of stretching and contracting is imperative for leaders. While it may make sense to stretch ourselves in emergency situations, continually stretching is not a long-term solution for leadership. It's also not sustainable throughout a career. It's important to pay attention to your own rhythms and know whether you need to stretch or to contract. Sometimes the act of getting up to physically stretch helps you stretch mentally. Similarly, closing your eyes and taking a few deep breaths (contracting) allows you to cope with the stresses of the moment. Being able to identify when taking on new responsibilities is vital and when it is to our detriment is something all leaders need to practice.

Paying attention to the rhythms of your staff members is also critical. How can you help people stretch their skills and grow in their work as people? When can you help people pull back for a time, to contract for a reprieve? Giving people a chance to briefly stop stretching helps them be able to meet the next round of challenges.

Stretching to the Future

One of my all-time favorite courses was a graduate course I took as part of my doctoral work. Entitled "Leadership, Literature, and the Individual," it was taught as part of the Masters in Business Administration. We studied leadership by reading novels. Of course, I loved it. The premise of the course was outlined on the syllabus as follows:

"This course begins with the postulate that novels and plays are among the world's greatest instruments of education… When we allow the skilled writer to take us on a journey into the minds of fictitious characters, then we must visualize and imagine the outcomes of those encounters and thereby learn about ourselves. This ability to imagine the outcome of future interactions seems to be one of the characteristics of a good leader."

This is part of what we mean when we say we want leaders who have a vision, people who can imagine the future. Even more, we want leaders who can imagine a new future, who can stretch their imaginations into new places, new interactions, and empathize with the experiences and responses of others.

In yoga, we practice stretching to allow us to increase our range of motion and our ability to sit quietly in meditation. In leadership, we stretch to increase our skills. We work to extend the range of options we have to respond to the many situations we face. And we reach to improve our ability to imagine new ways to serve our organizations and the people they are designed to serve.

We need leaders who can help us learn to amplify our imaginations and develop new ideas for a variety of possible new futures. Facing the future is always challenging. Imagining a future can be daunting, but it's possible if we stretch.

It's within a leader's scope to also stretch back to help others come forward. Leaders help others stretch toward a new way of doing and being. Yoga emboldens us to trust our ability to stretch safely and then, as leaders, guide others safely into the unknown.

Questions for Reflection

- ❋ What are your habits of movement, behavior, or thought? Are those habits helping you or hindering you? It may have been helpful to have these habits and not think about them, but is that still true?

- ❋ Will these habits support you as you stretch to make the changes organizations need or will they leave you behind? Where do you need to look to find new ways of thinking and doing for your organization and your leadership?

- ❋ Are there ways you need to learn to stretch physically?

Changing your physical behaviors supports you on multiple levels.

- ❋ Are there ways you need to stretch mentally? Are you working to learn new things? Are you reading outside your field? Who are you listening to, having lunch with, learning from?

- ❋ What about emotionally and spiritually? Have you developed habitual ways of experiencing the world around you?

- ❋ Are you more closed-off from emotion than you would like to be?

- ❋ What practices can help you stretch and grow your emotional and spiritual engagement with the world?

Stretch Practices

Try the Forward Bend

Give yourself the gift of a mid-day break with the relaxed energy of *Uttanasana*. If you practice each day, you'll have less need for sugar or caffeine when you are tired. Additionally, you'll begin to stretch the muscles along your entire back, from head to heel. Eventually, you'll be able to put your hands on the floor. This is a kind of flexibility that has a great deal of functional usefulness and is especially important as we grow older.

Learn Something New, Try Something New
Whether you select something directly in your employment or start a new hobby, pick something new to learn or do. It could be learning a new software, creating a program, or identifying a new service to design. Take a bit of a risk. Or perhaps you decide to throw yourself into a new kind of exercise or hobby. Try something that scares you. If you don't want to jump out of an airplane, maybe zip lining or a high ropes course is enough. Push yourself, safely and thoughtfully, to stretch and try something new.

Uttanasana (Standing Forward Bend)

The forward bend – *Uttanasana* – is a posture we do many times in our lives, but unless we have practiced yoga, we rarely think much about it. Most of the time, it is a utilitarian posture, something we do to allow us to achieve something else. That something else may be picking something off the floor or stretching to tie our shoes, but rarely do we think about what is happening when we do a forward bend.

Generally, if we are asked to touch our toes, we simply bend over with rounded back to do so, or if our hamstrings are tight, we let our arms dangle in the vicinity of knees, shins, or ankles. Yoga teaches us a different way to bend forward.

To perform Uttanasana, first come into Mountain Pose. Once you are aligned in Mountain, bring your hands to your hips and, keeping your back elongated, begin to bend forward from your hips as you exhale. If at any point, you feel your back begin to round, stop and breathe. As you inhale, lengthen your back. Imagine stretching from your hips forward and as you exhale, continue to hinge forward. Practice this extension and gentle forward bend a couple of times until you can go no further with a straight back. At that point, round over and relax on your next exhalation.

Try to keep your knees straight, but if that causes strain in your back or your hamstrings, let your knees soften slightly. Place your hands on the floor, or your ankles or shins, for additional support and allow your head to droop toward the floor.

An alternate, even more relaxing version of this posture has you clasp your elbows with your hands over your head and let the weight of your arms help you deepen the pose.

If you want, deepen the stretch by bending your knees enough to allow you to touch the floor or flatten your hands on the floor if you are already there. Now, gently push your thigh bones back toward the wall behind you. Most of us, when we bend over, push our buttocks back to serve as a counterbalance. This means that our legs are no longer fully perpendicular to the floor. This adjustment through the knees and thighs shifts our weight and changes the relationship of our legs to the floor and to the rest of our body. It makes the pose deeper and allows us to come closer to the ideal of the top of our head pointing directly to the floor.

Enjoy the pose. If you are struggling to breathe deeply because your abdomen is contracted, imagine breathing into the back of your lungs. This will help your ribs expand and loosen your breathing.

When you are ready to stand, roll slowly up one vertebra at a time back into Mountain Pose. Most of my teachers have likened this action to pearls being slid onto a string one at a time. Your head should come up last and just as slowly. Standing up gradually takes care of your back and keeps you from getting dizzy, though you might feel slightly light-headed. This is not the only way to come out of this posture, but it is the safest.

One of the reasons I like this pose so much is that it is both relaxing and energizing. Standing in forward bend for several breaths allows our hearts to ease and nourishes our brain physically. As a result, when we stand back up, we often feel a calm, alert energy. Getting out of our chairs, stretching toward the sky and then carefully coming into and holding a forward bend is a great mid-afternoon pick-me-up. And I've never met anyone who couldn't use a bit of an energy boost.

Practice 7

Managing Your Energy

What did you think of when you read that this chapter was going to focus on energy? For many people, it is an immediate wish for more energy. If that was your instant reaction, it may be that you understand energy as the ability to get up and get something done. In that case, it has a mechanical meaning. It's the capacity for doing work.

Physicists might consider energy as potential and break it down into types – kinetic, thermal, electrical, chemical, and nuclear to name a few. For people who practice yoga, the answer is a bit more esoteric. In yoga, *prana* is vital energy, our life force. In this framework, "Doing yoga maximizes your body's flow of the universal life force, giving you better health and increased vitality" (Budilovsky, p. 4). Understanding the different ways we experience energy, what brings us energy, and what drains us of energy is a critical self-care practice.

For me, water represents energy in all of its manifestations. The crashing of waves is a vibrant, exciting, and sometimes overwhelming kind of energy. But the water in slow rivers and still ponds is a calm, peaceful energy. For many people, myself included, being around either version of water is centering. Rushing floodwaters and relentless tsunamis show us the power of water while a soaking rain brings new life to parched land. Over time, water can even erode the hardest of rocks.

Water is a visible form of energy that can help us understand the variable nature of energy. Through the practice of yoga, we can become aware of the flexible nature of our own energy and how we can manage and even shift our energy when necessary. If we are tired (lacking energy), we can choose backbends for their revitalizing effect. Conversely, we can choose forward bends for calming energy to help us through difficult situations or aid us in finding sleep. When we are anxious or frenetic, we can turn to yoga to change that energy to something more helpful and directed. When we are lethargic, we can use yoga as way to get our energy moving. If we are sad or overwhelmed, yoga can help us understand and acknowledge our emotions and ride the wave rather than be swamped by it.

In this way, yoga becomes both a practice for our own health as individuals and our community and leadership roles. When we are better able to understand and manage our energy, we can more effectively support those around us. We are less likely to cause difficulties for the people with whom we are working. When we manage our energy, rather than allowing ourselves to become overwhelmed by it, it becomes calming and life-giving.

Bending Over Backwards

I looked up the phrase "to bend over backward" on several websites in preparation to write about backbends and found the general meaning consistent – to expend effort to make sure something happens, or more specifically, to expend effort to help someone else accomplish something. In every case, there was a sense of effort, sometimes great effort.

And I understand that. I'm not great at backbends. Never have been. I've never been all that flexible. Plus, true backbends do require effort. To do a backbend safely, one needs arm strength for support. To bend over backwards from the standing position (rather than pushing up from the floor), one needs core strength. Beyond that, we don't know what is behind us, so when you bend backwards, you are moving into the unknown and that can be scary.

Before I studied yoga, everything I knew about backbends told me that I didn't want to do them. However, there is good news since there are, in fact, many types and levels of backbends. And, contrary to the meaning of the cliché, such exercises come with great benefits.

Backbends of all kinds and at all levels help us breathe more deeply, which moves more oxygen through the body, leading to more physical energy. They work to counteract the hunched postures that come from peering at a computer screen or, even worse, looking down at a small phone or tablet. Backbends bring "vitality and lightness to your body and mind" (Sparrow, L. & P. Walden, p. 25), something I suspect we all would enjoy.

I eventually learned to do a backbend – over an exercise ball. It's still my favorite way to do one. The support allows me to relax into the posture so I'm not worrying about collapsing or hurting my back. However, it does rob me of the strength-building opportunities of the pose, despite still needing core and leg strength to keep myself from rolling off the ball. Even though I lose some of the benefits, I am able to experience the effects of a full stretch of the front side of the body which really doesn't happen any other way.

After completing my backbend over an exercise ball at a gym, I was approached by an older coach who worked primarily with boxers. "Well, it looks like you have the flexibility thing workin'. Gymnastics in your teens?" he asked.

I laughed. "Nope. Yoga in my forties."

He grinned and said, "That'll do." And he's right, that'll do. Finding a way to try postures that you have always thought were beyond you is another important part of the practice of yoga.

Let's take all of these ideas into the practice of leadership. Where are you bending over backward to help people? Is this a positive part of your leadership, stemming from compassion, care, and support? Or is it actually a habit of spending great effort to help others when they should be doing the work themselves?

Perhaps you are telling yourself that you or your organization can't do something. Take a moment to really think about it. Is it your fear of the unknown or are you afraid you or your organization won't have the flexibility to accomplish this challenge? If this fear of or actual lack of flexibility is keeping you from doing good work, perhaps there are supports like my balance ball that can increase your ability to take this step into the unknown. For example, a common fear cited among people is public speaking. Practice using a teleprompter or even join a Toastmasters class or workshop to find support. Finding ways to try something new brings new energy to individuals and organizations.

Energy Flow

I was given a great gift early in my career when I had the opportunity to take a workshop on the Myers-Briggs Type Indicator (MBTI). I was to join the Office of the Dean of Students at The University of Texas at Austin (UT) in a few weeks, but I spent one day of my apartment-hunting trip with my new colleagues-to-be as we learned about ourselves and each other through the MBTI. I learned many things that day. We had a truly excellent facilitator work with us and I use what I learned about the MBTI to this day. But what may be the most important item I learned from this workshop was a new understanding about energy.

The MBTI teaches us that the concept of extroversion and introversion is, in part, about energy. Simplified greatly, Myers-Briggs explained something I had felt but never understood before. The question of whether one is an introvert or an extrovert isn't a question of shyness, but about energy.

For introverts, engaging with people is an energy outflow. Extroverts, on the other hand, find that being around people brings them energy. Our facilitator illustrated this in a simple way. He divided us into groups and told us to plan a party. Some of the groups planned all-out bashes with music, people, food, and drink. Others prepared small get-togethers with friends around a table, potluck style. The differences were striking. Unbeknownst to us, the facilitator had created groups of extroverts, the large-party people, and introverts, the small-party people. Neither group was all that interested in the other's party.

For most of my career, I have worked a very extroverted job. I love my career. But my introversion is why at the end of a day full of people, I like a bit of quiet time or on a weekend, I have no real need to go to a party. Being with people all day, being 'on' all day is an energy outflow for me. Knowing that helps me make time for recovery. It helps me explain why I need time to myself and allows me to better understand my colleagues who operate differently.

People who are even more introverted than I am might not like many of the jobs I've had over the years because it was more energy outflow than they could manage. People who are more extroverted may struggle having the energy they need while they are working on long, solitary tasks like writing a report or dissertation. They'll often want to party on Friday night even if it was a busy week.

Although this is just one, very simplified aspect of introversion/extroversion, even understanding this much can help us understand why our energy is depleted at different times and in different situations. Yoga teaches us simple ways to change our energy when stress is too much. Understanding what energizes or drains us can help keep ourselves from getting overly stressed.

Having personal and social awareness of what drains or energizes you or your colleagues is an important leadership skill. Backbends and forward bends, to name simple postures, are ways to bring another version of energy management to our lives and leadership.

Create Space

You might be wondering what the idea of creating space has to do with the topic of managing energy. The idea comes from Echkart Tolle, who once wrote, "When you get into your car, shut the door, and be there for just half a minute. Breathe, feel the energy inside your body, look around at the sky, the trees. The mind might tell you, 'I don't have time.' But that's the mind talking to you. Even the busiest person has time for thirty seconds of space."

Creating even that tiny amount of space in our day, taking a moment to pause, giving ourselves the gift of time to experience the world around us is one way to manage our energy.

For five years, I commuted 55 miles each way from the campus of The University of Texas at San Antonio (UTSA) to our home outside of New Braunfels, Texas. Now, after working from home for four years, I find the commute from the back of the house to my office in the front of the house is lovely and it takes no time at all. But there were positive aspects to my lengthy drives that I do miss on occasion.

What I enjoyed about traveling between San Antonio and New Braunfels was the mental space in between campus and home. I listened to and enjoyed a variety of podcasts, which I have to now make time for. On the way to work, I had time to think about the day to come before anyone could grab my attention away. It was a chance to prioritize, set an intention, think through a difficult discussion, and to prepare myself.

On the way home, I had time to process what had happened during the day and decompress. I also had time to notice the changing seasons, subtle as that change is in Central Texas. That physical space gave me mental and emotional space. That bit of space, even if it's only a few minutes, is important in managing your energy.

Whatever your commute or lack of one, try to think about ways to create even 30 seconds of space in your day. Take a moment to breathe deeply and notice the world around you.

To mix metaphors, creating this mental space helps us stay grounded when everything around us is topsy-turvy. What works for you may not work for others, but I wonder how the energy in our lives could shift if we found a way for everyone to find 30 seconds in the day to "be there for just half a minute."

Slowing Down Faster

"Slow down, Sarah. Slow down, Sarah. Slow down *faster*, Sarah."

These words, said in a tone of absolute calm, were quietly uttered by my husband as our daughter, a new driver, hurtled (at least it seemed that way from the back seat) downhill toward a red light at a busy Austin intersection. "Slow down faster, Sarah," instantly became a family classic to be repeated at various times over the years.

Of course, I love the paradox — the idea of going slower faster tickles my sense of ridiculousness and illustrates the various conundrums we face in our lives. It also speaks to the combination of energy and calm we often need to create in our lives and in our work.

Parker Palmer tells a great story about this paradox in his description of a heart surgeon working with a new resident who says during surgery, "Now at this point, you have exactly 60 seconds to reconnect this artery or the patient will die. So, what you must do is go very slowly." No matter how many times I hear or share this story, the idea of it still awes me. I'm amazed by the idea of holding someone's life in your hands with a deadline — but you can't rush.

Most of the work we do is never immediately life or death, so it ought to be simple to slow down. But it isn't, is it?

So often in our lives, we get caught up in the urgency of the moment, thinking something has to be done now only to find mistakes in the rushed-through product. We all know the frustration so common it's a cliché — "your poor planning is not my emergency." Those *emergencies* we rush through with a bad attitude.

But what might happen if we took a moment to slow down and, instead of rushing from one task to another, quit trying to be champion multitaskers. Then we could pay attention to the one thing in front of us and do it slowly and very well. Or, even more importantly, we could stop and listen carefully to the person in front of us. We might find we could slowly get more done and done well with less stress.

As you face major tasks at work and home, remember the words of my husband and the heart surgeon and slow down a little rather than trying to run faster. Then as we hurtle toward the unknown, maybe we can calmly help each other slow down faster and enjoy the ride.

Questions for Reflection

❀ How well do you understand what energizes you? What drains your energy and saps your mental fortitude?

Take some time to pay attention to the way you feel after working on different kinds of tasks, during and after interactions with individuals and groups of people, and solo activities. Understanding your varying responses to situations can help manage your energy throughout the day. If you have a series of appointments or tasks that you know will leave you drained, plan for something reenergizing at the end of the day. If your schedule allows you the time, insert reenergizing activities.

If a day of nonstop appointments wears on you, perhaps schedule lunch to be a solo affair. Conversely, if your day is comprised of nothing but tedious and dull work, make a lunch date with a couple of friends. A day that is full of energizing activities may be fun, but perhaps you need a moment of calm to maintain your energy throughout the day.

Taking the time to understand your own energy patterns can help support your ability to stay healthy and active, all the while finishing everything on your to-do list.

❀ What do you understand about the energy of the people around you?

Perceiving and understanding that we each hold and experience energy differently is not only advantageous to completing tasks with which we've been charged. It's also a part of leadership. Observing the rhythms of your work environment and the variations that reverberate throughout the organization can open your mind to a new type of self-awareness.

In most organizations, stressful times happen when everyone is rushing to meet a deadline, or when a supervisor is pushing subordinates too hard, or even when, despite a reasonable workload, office morale is generally low. Understanding those rhythms allows you to better bolster the work of others. A word of support or appreciation may be all someone needs to be reenergized to continue meeting current demands. But to meet the needs of others, we have to pay attention to what they are experiencing and then determine the best way to help them manage their workflow and their energy flow.

Energy Practice

Creating Space

Those of you who have small children at home or complicated lives taking care of parents or other family or friends may be shaking your heads right now because you can't imagine doing this. Of course, that probably means you need to find ways to do this most of all. To have the energy to do all that is asked of us as humans and as leaders, we need to create space in some way. Maybe parents can sit for a few moments with their children, or caretakers with their loved ones. It's not alone time, but time to listen to them.

Perhaps you can take some time in the evening to watch the sunset or look at stars. Can you teach the people you share space with a ritual of quiet time together? Thirty seconds may be all they can manage, but it's a start. How might you create 30 seconds of space for yourself? How might you create space for the others around you? How might you teach or encourage them to create space and quiet?

As a leader, what would it be like to create space for the people in your organization? Where can you give them permission to take some time during the day, during a busy week, to have a moment of calm? How can you help them find practices to support their work and help them manage their energy — finding calm when it's hectic or energy when the work is hard and draining?

Anuvittasana (Standing Backbend)

Anuvittasana, Standing Backbend, is a simple way to gain the benefits from backbends before you are ready to try the full pose. Additionally, it's something you can do at any time, in most any place. In reality, we often take this pose naturally after we've been sitting for a long time.

As usual, begin in Mountain Pose. After you have worked to ground your feet and legs solidly, pay special attention to your spine and torso. Inhale deeply and lengthen your spine, creating space between each vertebra. Imagine

you are being gently pulled by the string attached to your head. Roll your shoulder blades back and down.

After you are comfortably standing in Mountain Pose, inhale deeply and begin to arch the upper part of your back. Bring your hands up to your hips/lower back, with your fingers pointed down for support *or* bring your hands over your head – whichever is more comfortable. Just as we did with Forward Bend, we'll work with the rhythm of the breath.

Inhale and arch backwards.
Exhale and relax.

We call it a backbend and it is, but paradoxically, the best way to practice this pose is by focusing on your chest. Imagine the arch you are creating as opening the front of the spine and lifting your chest up. Envision your heart lifting toward the sky. Feel your ribs expanding with each breath and your shoulder blades naturally moving toward each other – not being forced together, but naturally coming together as your heart lifts. Think about stretching the front of your body as you gently arch your back.

Once you have extended to your longest stretch, stay there for two or three breaths and then slowly come forward, back to Mountain Pose. Like Forward Bend, coming upright can make you feel a bit light-headed. So, stand quietly for a moment in Mountain and pay attention to your energy. Notice what has and hasn't changed.

For most people, this expansion of the chest and opening up of the heart is deeply nourishing. As a result, it's a great pose for anytime during the day when your back would like a little stretch and you could use a little boost.

Practice 8

Learning to Twist

"Nah, yoga's not for me. I've never been flexible," may be the number one excuse I hear from people who are unwilling to try a yoga class. One of the reasons people think they aren't flexible enough to try yoga is the mistaken idea that they have to be able to twist themselves into one of those postures where you can't quite figure which leg is which. Of course, the person who can do that is either naturally very limber or, more likely, someone who has spent time on their practice of yoga and has become more flexible over time.

But we aren't required to be highly flexible to participate in and benefit from yoga any more than we are required to be perfect before we can become leaders. If we are open to the lessons of yoga and organizational life, each of us can become more flexible physically and in our leadership.

"I'm so glad to hear you talk about being introverted. I've never thought I could be a vice president as an introvert," said a participant in a leadership institute. "I can't/I don't want to… because you have to____," is a formulation of a limiting belief. While there are many sources and causes of limiting beliefs, I've often found it's our understanding of an idea, concept, or activity that is limited.

For example, I said for years that I wasn't creative. One day when I said it again to my husband, his response was, "What do you mean you aren't creative? When someone comes to you with a problem, you come up with 15 different solutions. You're one of the most creative people I know."

My immediate response was, "That's not creativity. That's just problem-solving." And in that moment, I understood that the problem wasn't my lack of creativity, but my limited definition of the concept.

Or perhaps it's not our definition that's the problem. Perhaps it's the ability to see our own strengths and weaknesses clearly. Here's another such "aha moment" of mine. I was a participant in a week-long leadership institute and one of the activities was to form a line by linking hands with six or seven other participants to become a rope. Each team was given an enlarged picture from the Boy Scouts manual. The page was used to teach the tying of knots and our task was to tie our rope into each knot.

My immediate comment was, "Oh, no. I'm not good at tasks like this. I don't do this spatial recognition thing well."

Thirty minutes later, after our team solved all three puzzles first, one of my teammates turned to me and said, "You do realize you're the reason we won, right? You guided us through every one of those knots." What fascinates me about this is that if she had not said something to me, I wouldn't have seen it. I would have walked away with my limiting belief about my skills intact in spite of the fact that it was completely wrong. What other tasks or opportunities have I walked away from because I was sure I couldn't do them?

Maybe the problem with our idea of flexibility is not our ability or inability to touch our toes, but our understanding of what it means to be flexible. Perhaps there's something about one person's individual body mechanics that makes toe-touching more possible for them. Or the opposite could be true. There actually is something about our body design that makes touching our toes more difficult or even impossible for us. That doesn't mean we aren't flexible in other ways or able to do other types of postures. Expanding our understanding of what it means to be physically flexible opens us to the idea that we're actually quite flexible, we just can't touch our toes.

Similarly, maybe it's not that we *can't* be leaders, but that we hold a limited understanding of what leadership is or what skills leaders need. A broader understanding of leadership could allow us to see that we have been leading for some time, whether or not we have a title. Recognizing that we have a limited belief about what leaders do and look like helps us see people who are leading in non-traditional and creative ways.

When we hear ourselves say, "I can't, because..." perhaps we need to alter our paradigm, change our perspective. Are the limitations we place on ourselves socially or personally implemented? Are they accurate? Do the physical or mental constraints we think we're under actually exist?

What if we take our ideas and twist them around a bit to see if they are too limited or too rigid? Maybe the challenge with our mental, emotional, or physical flexibility isn't in our skills, but in our ideas and perceptions.

Twists and Turns

Developing our ability to handle life's twists and turns is an important self-care practice. Understanding our body's ability to be flexible supports us in meeting the wide variety of mental and emotional challenges we face each day. In a similar way, our mind's ability to adjust to circumstances helps us remember our body is capable of moving in new and different ways, no matter our age or physical ability.

Yoga twists help us develop a strong, supple spine which allows our movements to be more fluid and supports us in all that we do. But it is important to remember that too abrupt a twist can be harmful. Forcing our body into a movement or pose before it is ready and able is harmful. Cranking our necks around rather than gently moving them hurts.

Yoga teacher and author Gary Kraftsow explains the need for care this way, "[T]he key to twisting is the ability to control rotation from the musculature of the abdomen and spine, rather than through the force of leverage generated by the musculature of the shoulder and arms and/or pelvis and legs" (p. 61).

In other words, we achieve healthy spinal twists not by forcing ourselves into the turn, but by gently working our way there from our core. Only then can we use our strength (arms and legs) to help us hold or deepen a position. Learning to twist in a gentle healthy way develops flexibility to be ready to move quickly with less harm in an emergency situation.

In the same way, cultivating an open and yielding mind and spirit permits us to handle even the most unexpected twists that life sends our way. Yoga teacher Rodney Yee likens such movements to willow branches, explaining that, "[T]wists allow you to be soft, fluid, and organic in our body movements. When you use force in a twist, it reveals how your mind is often directed and determined, reminding you to lead more from your center - your belly - and simply observe from your mind" (Yee, p. 257).

Take a moment to transfer that idea from the physical to the mental. Think about the way it feels when you are unsure but take an action any way. There are the times when people, circumstances, or your own fears push you to act (forced action). Compare this with the times when your action comes from your values, your sense that the timing is right, or you have been able to work with others to build a consensus. There's a marked difference in your confidence that you are making the best decision possible, isn't there?

The lessons yoga has to teach us – of twisting, moving from our center – remind us to respond to the challenges of life and leadership by moving from our core values and our knowledge of what is important.

As the experienced yogis who have learned to contort in amazing ways by developing their ability to twist and turn, our regular practice of responding to the adversities of life in healthy, value-based ways prepares us for the more difficult times. It won't make the problems less challenging or easier to solve, but it may help you feel more confident in your decisions and more trusting of your ability to embrace the changes.

Twists and turns will always come, but we can learn to move into them with suppleness and openness to avoid coiling ourselves into unhappy knots.

Standing Tall

But do we really want leaders with supple spines? Our metaphors might tell us otherwise. Having no backbone means you don't have the courage to do what is necessary. We encourage people to stiffen their spines when we want them to be courageous, strong, or to stand up for what they believe. Those certainly sound like virtues and they are, but it's possible to take a good thing too far, isn't it? And I think we have a limited idea of what it takes to 'stand tall,' particularly for our leaders.

When we talk about standing ramrod straight, I picture a person who fears the uncertainties of flexibility, someone who may be unable to admit to human error and weaknesses, and who, therefore, has a limited idea of leadership. Of course, we need leaders who are strong and have the courage of their convictions, but personally, I prefer working with leaders who have both the courage to be strong and the flexibility to change. I favor leaders who want to act in alignment with their values, but also have the humility to be willing and able to listen to other points of view.

To accomplish a yoga twist safely, we must first lengthen our spine and breathe deeply, which sounds to me like what we intuitively do when facing something challenging. To accomplish that move safely, we must pay attention to the messages from our bodies, moving smoothly and confidently while remaining alert for any resistance.

This seems to me to be a good metaphor for leadership. We stand or sit tall and supple, rather than rigid and unyielding when we know who we are, what we believe in, and how we can best support ourselves and our organizations. We have to keep breathing, taking care of ourselves and others as we face the challenges organizations and communities experience. And we need to remember, while we may be able to force our way through to solutions, often that's not the best for the long term, for ourselves, and for others.

If we work to establish a leadership style that doesn't confuse rigidity with strength or suppleness with weakness, we can develop the ability to move more easily with changing circumstances. We are also better able to see and appreciate the variety of talents and skills people bring with them, which allows us the flexibility to share the work of leadership.

It is through this limber leadership that we create a healthier, more sustainable style of leadership for ourselves and our organizations.

Questions for Reflection

❀ What beliefs do you have about your abilities and skills? Are those beliefs supporting or limiting you in your understanding of self-care or leadership? Are those beliefs helping you try new things, accept new challenges, or respond to life's challenges in a healthy, supple, flexible way?

❀ When you have opportunities to try something new, do you embrace them or shy away?

❀ What is your usual response to a challenge or problem? If your answer is that you like new challenges and solving problems, stop to ask the next question: are there categories of challenges and problems that you prefer not to take on?

❀ Are there areas that you traditionally turn away from?

Twist Exercises

Once you have answered those questions for yourself as honestly as you can, find a trusted friend and ask them to share their ideas about your skills and abilities. They may list some that never occurred to you. Be prepared – they may tell you that you need practice in something you thought you were doing well.

When you face new opportunities or challenges, try out a different response than your traditional one. If you usually solve things on your own, ask for help. If you tend to rely on a group of friends or colleagues, try to find your own solution first or invite someone new into the process. Find ways to recognize your habits and make even a little turn to something new and different. Cultivating options for meeting life's challenges and opportunities is a form of flexibility that we all can benefit from.

Parivrtta Sukhasana **(Easy Twist Pose)**

Sit with your legs crossed in front you. This is Easy Twist Pose or *Parivrtta Sukhasana.* Inhale deeply, lengthening your spine as you do so. Press your right hand into the floor behind your right hip to help you sit tall with your spine perpendicular to the floor (rather than leaning back slightly.)

As you exhale, begin to gently turn your belly button toward your right leg. Inhale and lengthen your spine.

Exhale slowly and gently turn your lower rib cage to your right. Imagine that you are working your way up a spiral stair case, one step at a time. Inhale and lengthen your spine.

Exhale and gently turn your chest to the right. Inhale and lengthen your spine.

Exhale and gently turn your shoulders and then let your head float through a turn to the right as far as it's comfortable. Inhale and lengthen your spine.

Continue to gently deepen the twists with each exhalation and lengthen your spine with each inhalation.

Optional: Place your left had on your right thigh just above your knee and use your hands and arms to deepen your twist. Only do this as long as it feels comfortable. Never begin the twist using your hands.

When you have completed a few deep inhalations and exhalations, release your hands as you exhale and turn back to center. Sit with your eyes closed or look down at the floor for a moment to feel the effects of the pose and let your spine and muscles relax. Then change the cross of your legs – if it was right over left, shift to left over right and repeat the step-by-step process.

Don't be surprised if one side is tighter than the other. Listen to your body and only proceed as deeply as feels comfortable. The key to making this pose safe and comfortable is to make each movement slow and easy.

Practice 9

Relaxing and Reflecting

Savasana is one of the most important poses in yoga. It is traditionally the final pose to any yoga class – and the one most misunderstood by people new to yoga. Like seeing a room of people "doing nothing but standing" when a class is practicing Mountain Pose, people often joke that yoga classes end with nap time. But it doesn't take many classes before such skeptics begin to revise their perception as they experience the challenges and benefits of what often becomes their favorite pose.

Several of my yoga teachers often explained that the postures we are most reluctant to try are the ones we will benefit from the most. Our very resistance to the pose is a hint that it touches on areas – physical, emotional, or mental – that are most difficult for us. In the same way, I find many people are resistant to the idea of making time for reflection. They don't have time for it; it's not useful; it's too time-consuming.

Yet, as mentioned in the second chapter, making time for reflection is an important component of self-awareness. In my experience, it may be the essential practice for self-care. Like that challenging yoga posture, understanding and moving through your resistance to this practice has the potential to bring great benefits over time.

Savasana (Corpse Pose)

First and foremost, the goal of *Savasana* is to "relax the body so completely that it becomes irrelevant, as it if were deceased. With the body 'gone,' the mind is set free to blossom" (Budilovsky, p. 197). This quote points us toward understanding the name of this pose which translates as Corpse Pose.

This idea of complete relaxation is one of the reasons this pose is often difficult to achieve and is one of the reasons the pose can be so challenging to new students. Of all the poses, *Savasana* is counter to almost every cultural norm in the United States. Lying down, closing one's eyes, and letting oneself relax completely in a

room full of people, often strangers, is not our usual way of being in community. It can be difficult to relax in that environment. Many new students lie there feeling tense, staring at the ceiling and wondering how long they have to keep this up. Other students might fall asleep the minute they lie down. Neither is the right way to practice the pose. "The essence of Savasana is to relax with attention, that is, to remain conscious and alert while still being at ease. Remaining aware while relaxing can help you begin to notice and release long-held tensions in your body and mind" (Costello, "The Subtle Struggle of Savasana").

Of course, like so much of a yoga practice, simply reaching a point where we feel comfortable with the pose or the practice doesn't mean it won't be challenging tomorrow. Yoga is thoroughly grounded in the moment and in what we bring to its discipline each day.

Some days we relax immediately into the pose while others, we struggle not to squirm and fidget – even if we are in the same spot, in the same room, at the same time of day. Some days, we are able to let our mind calm and other days, we learn all over again what it means to have a monkey mind – unsettled, restless, chasing after every thought that appears.

"Perhaps the most compelling reason for us Westerners to practice *shavasana* (alternative spelling) is that it simply brings more peace into our lives. Imagine yourself calmer and more clear-headed, able to take any situation in stride, handle any emergency with unruffled confidence. The regular practice of *shavasana* can give you this gift" (Budilovsky, p. 204).

Savasana brings us the chance to practice the paradoxical gifts of yoga. Lying relaxed on the floor, doing nothing, is an active way to bring more peace and calm into our lives. It is a gift we give ourselves.

Living the Practice

Like yoga, leadership is also a practice grounded in the moment. Yes, we plan ahead, strategize, and imagine new futures, but none of that matters if our day-to-day, moment-to-moment practice of leadership isn't effective.

During my senior year in high school, I took a class that was designed to help us be successful in college. During the first half of the year, we learned to touch-type. Yes, this was a long time ago, so I learned to type on a manual machine, which included the fun action of punctuating the end of a line with a whack to the return lever.

In the second half of the class, we learned a modified form of shorthand called Notehand. The idea was that we would be able to take notes quickly and easily in class and afterward transcribe and annotate those notes. I tried it for a short while during my first semester and then gave up. I wish I had understood then why this was such a great idea.

As a busy administrator, I experienced firsthand why taking some time after a meeting or a class to go over your notes is so important. It was easy to tell when I had had a day that was scheduled with back-to-back meetings. At the end of the day, my desk was full of memo pads and notes. During each meeting, I would take notes, toss the pad on the desk, grab another pad, and head to the next meeting. At the end of the day, I had a desk full of notes and almost no memory of what I had just added to my to-do list. Nothing had gotten past my short-term memory. And by the next day, I almost didn't know what the notes meant. The reason was simple – I never stopped to capture what was important.

I certainly didn't stop to process what had worked or gone poorly during a meeting; I just kept moving from one task to the next. Not a good practice for leadership or self-care. I learned compensatory note-taking processes like big stars, circles, arrows, or directions to myself, but struggled with doing what I knew I had to do – stop for a just a few moments and let myself think about what was important from each meeting or conversation.

At the end of a meeting, leaders need to stop and reflect. Take five minutes to jot down tasks, questions, or ideas that came from the meeting to help you retrieve them later. At the end of a contentious discussion, taking time to reflect on all that just happened, accomplishments as well as setbacks, helps you be ready to face long-term goals and those that need immediate attention.

Simply, we need to bring the practice of *Savasana* into our daily routines. One of my teachers described the purpose of *Savasana* as a time to let the work of the class be absorbed into the body. It isn't enough to go through the motions of the class, even if you are moving mindfully. *Savasana* is a time to allow your body fully relax, allowing muscles, mind, and emotions to release what tension they've accumulated.

In our leadership practice, finding time to reflect on our work throughout the day allows us to remember what is important, not just what's on our to-do list. Finding time to reflect on the work at hand and contemplate the ways we can make that work matter is an essential leadership skill. Properly utilizing this time, forces us to meditate on what we learned, what was challenging, and where we need to follow up.

Did we make the best decision possible given the circumstances? Did we keep our organizational mission and vision in mind as we completed our work in each meeting and throughout the day?

What about our personal values? Were there places and times when there were conflicts between our personal values, organizational values, or the actions being taken? If so, what do you need to do next? What might you do next time to keep things more in alignment?

Taking the time to regularly reflect and analyze gives us the opportunity to make immediate changes or to handle matters differently the next time. This is self-care for leaders – paying attention, reflecting, and adjusting as needed, rather than looking back in dismay when things have gone too far awry to repair.

Ebb and Flow

In yoga classes, we learn to balance opposing forces through the postures we practice. We follow backbends that cultivate energy with forward bends that promote tranquility. Contractions – folding into ourselves – are balanced with extensions – reaching out, thus mirroring the natural ebb and flow of energy in our bodies, work, and lives.

Yoga encourages us to be aware of this natural rhythm, and over time, can teach us methods to understand our own feelings and reactions and find ways to guide our energy along different paths as needed. Understanding our need for interaction and time alone, being able to listen to anger, fear, and pain with compassion, and being able to step away to take care of oneself is the same practice.

When I teach yoga, I don't stand at the front of the room and do every pose. My preference is to demonstrate a pose and then watch the class. I'm looking for people who are struggling, who might benefit from a bit of coaching or a supportive prop, or for those who need a modification of the pose. I'm also watching the clock to make sure I'm managing time well. During *Savasana*, I'm guiding the relaxation and bringing people to a peaceful end. I'm teaching yoga, not practicing yoga.

What I didn't expect when I began teaching yoga was that I would feel just as good after teaching as I do after practicing it. While I don't get the same stretch or muscle workout, the focus of teaching the class, paying attention to the experiences of students, and slowing my breath during *Savasana*, work together.

In this way, teaching yoga is very much like leadership. A teacher's focus is like that of a leader – both internal and external. The focus is on the experience of each individual and of the class as a whole. But a teacher/leader who is not paying attention to their own experience or managing their energy can end up creating a class/work environment that is at best ineffective and at worst harmful.

Savasana as a yoga practice gives us the opportunity to experience the full benefit of a class or practice session. In the same way, self-awareness and making time for reflection is a self-care practice that allows us to be our best selves as leaders. Taking time to pay attention to our interactions with others, to our own physical, mental, and emotional reactions, gives us the opportunity to create the most effective leadership practices and experiences for ourselves and others.

We need leaders who are willing to take a deep breath in the middle of a difficult conversation or situation and help us get through it. *Savasana* isn't a nap or disengagement from the world. Rather, it is a practice of being aware of our thoughts but not being captured by them.

Self-care as a leadership practice gives us the ability to face all that comes at us, both the good and the bad. This is when we begin to understand that self-care as a leadership practice is not merely a set of actions aimed at making us feel better. Like *Savasana*, such practices are a way of integrating all that we know and all that we do to create both a healthy style of leadership and a healthy life.

Questions for Reflection

⚚ How do you practice reflection? If you don't, take some time to list the reasons why you don't. Now stop and realize that you just did some reflection.

❀ If you already find time for pausing and reflecting, further consider what you are doing. Is your practice still meeting your needs or should you alter it in any way?

❀ Does your practice include intentional moments of reflection during the day? Would such moments help? Take some time to think about how well your current practice is serving you.

Reflection Exercises

The best reflection activity is keeping a regular journal. In our work world, when we take time after a program or event to identify achievements and shortcomings, we often call this practice debriefing. Afterward, we determine the necessary changes to the process to not make the same mistakes next time. A journal allows us to do the same thing for ourselves.

If you don't like journaling, you can accomplish the same work while moving – running or walking *without* conversation, music, podcasts, or audiobooks. It is vital that we allow ourselves simply to *be*. Choosing a knotty problem to solve or letting your mind wander as you move are equally effective ways to help yourself understand what's important, what needs work, and what you yourself need to pay attention to as you move through your days.

Finding ways to insert moments of reflection and relaxation into your day is an amazingly powerful practice that cultivates long-term rewards.

Final Words

The New Colossus

Not like the brazen giant of Greek fame,
With conquering limbs astride from land to land;
Here at our sea-washed, sunset gates shall stand
A mighty woman with a torch, whose flame
Is the imprisoned lightning, and her name
Mother of Exiles. From her beacon-hand
Glows world-wide welcome; her mild eyes command
The air-bridged harbor that twin cities frame.
"Keep, ancient lands, your storied pomp!" cries she
With silent lips. "Give me your tired, your poor,
Your huddled masses yearning to breathe free,
The wretched refuse of your teeming shore.
Send these, the homeless, tempest-tost to me, I lift my lamp beside
the golden door!"

Emma Lazarus, 1883

My plans for March and April of 2020 included writing the first draft of this book. Of course, everything changed mid-March with the outbreak of COVID-19.

It was early one Friday morning and I was in a hotel room getting ready to head to the lovely Lady Bird Johnson Wildflower Center to spend half a day completing a professional development workshop for staff from The University of Texas at Austin. I had a moment to look at Twitter and saw an announcement saying that the campus would be closed that day since someone had tested positive for COVID-19. Spring Break started prematurely and I drove home early.

A week later, I started feeling ill. I spent the next two weeks in quarantine in the spare bedroom. Tests were few and far between then and my symptoms were mild with no lasting effects, so I still don't know whether I had COVID-19. I just know I felt miserable. The idea of writing a book that would be available several months in the future made no sense. So instead, I began writing blog posts and sharing them with readers of my weekly newsletter. Those posts became the first draft of this book.

Just like this book and my yoga classes, I began the series of blog posts promoting the importance of our breathing. Thus, in a stroke of cruel irony, I found myself in March and April writing about the significance of paying attention to our breathing as hospitals across the country and the world cried out for ventilators for the thousands of people who were struggling to breathe.

In June, the Leadership Yoga blog series was completed, but I found myself writing and reflecting again on the act of breathing as thousands across the world gathered together, accepting the risks of COVID-19, to echo the phrase "I can't breathe" in support of George Floyd, Eric Garner, and countless others who became the victims of police brutality.

And so, I end this book with a simple statement – we are all struggling to breathe. For some, the literal tightness in our chests may be caused by illness, anxiety, or injury – all of which make breathing difficult. Others may feel we are choking on injustice, sadness, and fear.

Like the pulse of our heartbeat, most of us take the ability to breathe for granted. It's not something we pay much attention to in the course of the normal day. But if 2020, a year filled with days that were not normal, has taught us anything, it is to listen to our own breathing. Cherish that ability to breathe. When you can, take a deep, belly breath and let it out slowly. Find your inner calm and move forward – move forward with your work, with your responsibilities, your protests, your ambitions, your life.

It was as I was reworking the blog posts into this text that I came to truly understand the most important message of the Leadership Yoga Workshop. If we want to lead, to make a difference in the world, we have to understand that this work takes time. In March, we responded to an emergency and took quick action, but the reality is that a pandemic is more than a short-term crisis. It is a long-term challenge which requires the ability to sustain our energy over weeks and months.

Leadership asks us to stay engaged over years, which means self-care is a necessity, not a luxury. Each of us has to find ways to stay healthy physically, mentally, and emotionally. I offer these ideas as ways to support you as you take care of yourself. After all, if you can't take care of yourself, how can you possibly take care of others?

Continuous, thoughtful self-care practices support strong leaders centered on serving, improving, and progressing.

Take care.

Bibliography

André, Christophe. "Proper Breathing Brings Better Health." *Scientific American.* January 15, 2019. https://www.scientificamerican.com/article/proper-breathing-brings-better-health/.

"Balance." *Lexico: Oxford English and Spanish Dictionary, Thesaurus, and Spanish-to-English Translator.* Accessed on November 2, 2020. https://www.lexico.com/en/definition/balance

Budilovsky, J. and E. Admason. *The Complete Idiot's Guide to Yoga.* New York: Alpha Books, 1998. P. 4, 197, 204.

Cameron, Julia. "Morning Pages." *The Artist's Way.* Accessed November 2, 2020. https://juliacameronlive.com/basic-tools/morning-pages/.

Carrico, M. et al. *Yoga Journal's Yoga: The Essential Beginner's Guide to Yoga for a Lifetime of Health and Fitness.* New York: Henry Holt & Co., 1997. P. 4, 18.

Carrol, C. & L. Kamata. *Partner Yoga: Making Contact for Physical, Emotional, and Spiritual Growth.* Rodale Books, 2000. P. 96, 133.

"Contemplative Pedagogy." *Columbia Center for Teaching and Learning.* Accessed November 2, 2020. https://ctl.columbia.edu/resources-and-technology/resources/contemplative-pedagogy/.

Costello, Nikki. "The Subtle Struggle of Savasana." November 14, 2013. YogaJournal.com. https://www.yogajournal.com/practice/corpse-pose.

Farhi, D. *The Breathing Book: Good Health and Vitality Through Essential Breath Work.* New York: Henry Holt and Company, 1996. P. XV, 87.

Goleman, D., R. Boyatzis, & A. McKee. *Primal Leadership: Realizing the Power of Emotional Intelligence.* Boston: Harvard Business School Press, 2002. P. 40.

Iyengar, B.K.S. *Light on Yoga.* New York: Schocken Books, 1976. P. 19.

Jami, Criss. "To share your weakness is to make yourself vulnerable; to make yourself vulnerable is to show your strength." Accessed November 2, 2020. Goodreads.com. https://www.goodreads.com/quotes/512034-to-share-your-weakness-is-to-make-yourself-vulnerable-to.

Joseph, Pilates. "Physical fitness is the first requisite of happiness." Accessed November 2, 2020. Quotefancy.com. https://quotefancy.com/joseph-pilates-quotes.

Kraftsow, g. *Yoga for Wellness.* New York: Penguin Compass, 1999. P. 61, 114.

Lang, James M. "Small Changes in Teaching: The First 5 Minutes of Class." January 11, 2016. *The Chronicle of Higher Education.* https://www.chronicle.com/article/small-changes-in-teaching-the-first-5-minutes-of-class/.

Matusak, L. *Finding Your Voice: Learning to Lead… Anywhere You Want to Make a Difference.* San Francisco: Jossey-Bass, 1997.

Palmer, P.J. *Let Your Life Speak: Listening for the Voice of Vocation.* San Francisco: Jossey-Bass, 2000. P. 78.

Schiffman, E. *Yoga: The Spirit and the Practice of Stillness.* New York: Pocket Books, 1996. P. 51-52.

Sparrowe, L. and P. Walden. *The Women's Book of Yoga and Health.* Boston: Shambhala, 2002. P. 25.

Tolle, Echkart. "When you get into your car, shut the door and be there for just half a minute. Breathe, feel the energy inside your body, look around at the sky, the trees. The mind might tell you, 'I don't have time.' But that's the mind talking to you. Even the busiest person has time for 20 seconds of space." Accessed November 2, 2020. BrainyQuote.com. https://www.brainyquote.com/quotes/eckhart_tolle _571577.

"Walking Is Falling." *Core Walking for Pain Relief.* Accessed November 2, 2020. https://corewalking.com/walking-is-falling/.

Yee, R. with N. Zolotow. *Yoga: The Poetry of the Body.* New York: Thomas Dunne Books, 2002. P. 257.

Zhu, Jessie. "Why Self-awareness Matters and How to Be More Self-aware." January 27, 2015. LinkedIn.com. https://www.linkedin.com/pulse/why-self-awareness-matters-how-more-self-aware-jessie-zhu/.

Acknowledgments

Writing a book is both a solitary venture and a collaborative effort that requires the engagement and support of many people. This book exists because so many people were willing to try an odd-sounding workshop – whoever heard of mixing leadership with yoga? – and then tell me it was helpful. Then there were the people who signed up to read daily newsletters of my findings as I explored this outlandish concept. Their feedback and support spurred me to action. Thank you to each of them.

Special thanks go to colleagues and friends who continue to be readers, editors, and cheerleaders – Sharon Justice, Sandi Rhoten, Corey Benson, and Edna Dominguez.

Thank you to Kara Scrivener of Emerging Ink Solutions for providing great editing, giving me deadlines and assignments, and keeping me on track through a pandemic and her own move to another state!

And to reiterate what I said in my very first book, in the sense of movie credits where the really important actor's name comes at the very end, thank you to my husband Peter Geenberg. Not only did he review and edit my work-a-day writings of proposals, blogs, and newsletters, but he has always supported me in every endeavor – and that support makes all the difference.

About the Author

Gage E. Paine is the founder of Gage Paine Consulting, a consulting firm designed to support higher education and non-profit leaders who want to make a difference in their organizations and communities. She brings to this work more than 30 years of experience in higher education, including service as a vice president for three universities – Trinity University, The University of Texas at San Antonio, and The University of Texas at Austin.

Known for her creativity, her use of dance, yoga, and poetry in workshops and speeches, and recognized nationally as a leader in higher education, she is sought after as a facilitator, leadership coach, and speaker. Her resumé lists more than 100 speeches, presentations, and panels including her talk at TEDxSanAntonio in 2012. She has taught undergraduate courses in leadership at both SMU and Trinity University in San Antonio.

In addition to yoga, Gage loves to read, knit, and dance. She lives in San Marcos, Texas with her husband of 31 years and their dog Wynne.

To learn more, visit: www.gagepaineconsulting.com